Certified Kubernetes Administrator (CKA) Study Guide
In-Depth Guidance and Practice

Benjamin Muschko

Beijing · Boston · Farnham · Sebastopol · Tokyo

Certified Kubernetes Administrator (CKA) Study Guide

by Benjamin Muschko

Published by O'Reilly Media, Inc., 1005 Gravenstein Highway North, Sebastopol, CA 95472.

O'Reilly books may be purchased for educational, business, or sales promotional use. Online editions are also available for most titles (*http://oreilly.com*). For more information, contact our corporate/institutional sales department: 800-998-9938 or corporate@oreilly.com.

Acquisitions Editor: John Devins
Development Editor: Michele Cronin
Production Editor: Beth Kelly
Copyeditor: Kim Wimpsett
Proofreader: Amnet Systems LLC

Indexer: Potomac Indexing, LLC
Interior Designer: David Futato
Cover Designer: Karen Montgomery
Illustrator: Kate Dullea

June 2022:   First Edition

Revision History for the First Edition

2022-06-09:   First Release

See *http://oreilly.com/catalog/errata.csp?isbn=9781098107222* for release details.

978-1-098-10722-2

[LSI]

Table of Contents

amount of example code from this book into your product's documentation does require permission. We appreciate, but generally do not require, attribution. An attribution usually includes the title, author, publisher, and ISBN. For example: "*Certified Kubernetes Administrator (CKA) Study Guide* by Benjamin Muschko (O'Reilly). Copyright 2022 Some Benjamin Muschko, 978-1-098-10722-2."

If you feel your use of code examples falls outside fair use or the permission given above, feel free to contact us at *permissions@oreilly.com*.

O'Reilly Interactive Katacoda Labs

Interactive Katacoda scenarios mimic real-world production environments and let you write and run code as you learn, right in your browser. The author has developed a collection of Katacoda scenarios to give you hands-on practice with the tools and practices outlined in this book. Visit *http://oreilly.com* for more information about our interactive content, to view the ebook format for this title, and also to learn about all our learning platform has to offer.

O'Reilly Online Learning

 For more than 40 years, *O'Reilly Media* has provided technology and business training, knowledge, and insight to help companies succeed.

Our unique network of experts and innovators share their knowledge and expertise through books, articles, and our online learning platform. O'Reilly's online learning platform gives you on-demand access to live training courses, in-depth learning paths, interactive coding environments, and a vast collection of text and video from O'Reilly and 200+ other publishers. For more information, visit *http://oreilly.com*.

How to Contact Us

Please address comments and questions concerning this book to the publisher:

O'Reilly Media, Inc.
1005 Gravenstein Highway North
Sebastopol, CA 95472
800-998-9938 (in the United States or Canada)
707-829-0515 (international or local)
707-829-0104 (fax)

Preface

Kubernetes, as a runtime and orchestration environment for microservices, is widely used among startups and large enterprises alike. As your organization ramps up on the number of applications, managing the Kubernetes clusters becomes a full-time job. That's the role of a Kubernetes administrator. The person responsible for this job ensures that each cluster is an operational state, scales up the cluster by onboarding nodes, upgrades the Kubernetes version of the nodes to incorporate patches and new features, and is in charge of a backup strategy for crucial cluster data. To help job seekers and employers have a standard means to demonstrate and evaluate proficiency in developing with a Kubernetes environment, the Cloud Native Computing Foundation (CNCF) developed the Certified Kubernetes Administrator (CKA) (*https://oreil.ly/Ds8nq*) program. To achieve this certification, you need to pass an exam.

There are two other Kubernetes certifications you can find on the CNCF web page. The Certified Kubernetes Application Developer (CKAD) (*https://oreil.ly/RxHwQ*) focuses on the developer-centric application of Kubernetes. The Certified Kubernetes Security Specialist (CKS) (*https://oreil.ly/53csH*) was created to verify the competence on security-based topics and requires a successful pass of the CKA exam before you can register. Passing the CKAD and CKS are not mandatory for taking the CKA exam.

In this study guide, I will explore the topics covered in the CKA exam to fully prepare you to pass the certification exam. We'll look at determining when and how you should apply the core concepts of Kubernetes to manage an application. We'll also examine the kubectl command-line tool, a mainstay of the Kubernetes engineer. I will also offer tips to help you better prepare for the exam and share my personal experience with getting ready for all aspects of it.

The CKA is different from the typical multiple-choice format of other certifications. It's completely performance based and requires you to demonstrate deep knowledge of the tasks at hand under immense time pressure. Are you ready to pass the test on the first go?

Who This Book Is For

The primary target group for this book is administrators who want to prepare for the CKA exam. The "exam details and resources" content covers all aspects of the exam curriculum, though basic knowledge of the Kubernetes architecture and its concepts is expected. If you are completely new to Kubernetes, I recommend reading *Kubernetes Up & Running* by Brendan Burns, Joe Beda, Kelsey Hightower, and Lachlan Evenson (O'Reilly) or *Kubernetes in Action* by Marko Lukša (Manning Publications) first.

What You Will Learn

The content of the book condenses the most important aspects relevant to the CKA exam. Cloud-provider-specific Kubernetes implementations like AKS or GKE do not need to be considered. Given the plethora of configuration options available in Kubernetes, it's almost impossible to cover all use cases and scenarios without duplicating the official documentation. Test takers are encouraged to reference the Kubernetes documentation (*https://oreil.ly/MoLjc*) as the go-to compendium for broader exposure.

The outline of the book follows the CKA curriculum to a T. While there might be a more natural, didactical structure for learning Kubernetes in general, the curriculum outline will help test takers prepare for the exam by focusing on specific topics. As a result, you will find yourself cross-referencing other chapters of the book depending on your existing knowledge level.

Be aware that this book covers only the concepts relevant to the CKA exam. Certain primitives that you may expect to be covered by the certification curriculum—for example, the API primitive Ingress—are not discussed. Refer to the Kubernetes documentation or other books if you want to dive deeper.

Practical experience with Kubernetes is key to passing the exam. Each chapter contains a section named "Sample Exercises" with practice questions. Solutions to those questions can be found in the Appendix.

Conventions Used in This Book

The following typographical conventions are used in this book:

Italic
> Indicates new terms, URLs, and email addresses.

`Constant width`
> Used for filenames, file extensions, and program listings, as well as within paragraphs to refer to program elements such as variable or function names, databases, data types, environment variables, statements, and keywords.

`Constant width bold`
> Shows commands or other text that should be typed literally by the user.

`Constant width italic`
> Shows text that should be replaced with user-supplied values or by values determined by context.

 This element signifies a tip or suggestion.

 This element signifies a general note.

 This element indicates a warning or caution.

Using Code Examples

The source code for all examples and exercises in this book is available on GitHub (*https://github.com/bmuschko/cka-study-guide*). The repository is distributed under the Apache License 2.0. The code is free to use in commercial and open source projects. If you encounter an issue in the source code or if you have a question, open an issue in the GitHub issue tracker (*https://oreil.ly/09Z7p*). I'll be happy to have a conversation and fix any issues that might arise.

This book is here to help you get your job done. In general, if example code is offered with this book, you may use it in your programs and documentation. You do not need to contact us for permission unless you're reproducing a significant portion of the code. For example, writing a program that uses several chunks of code from this book does not require permission. Selling or distributing examples from O'Reilly books does require permission. Answering a question by citing this book and quoting example code does not require permission. Incorporating a significant

Preface

Kubernetes, as a runtime and orchestration environment for microservices, is widely used among startups and large enterprises alike. As your organization ramps up on the number of applications, managing the Kubernetes clusters becomes a full-time job. That's the role of a Kubernetes administrator. The person responsible for this job ensures that each cluster is an operational state, scales up the cluster by onboarding nodes, upgrades the Kubernetes version of the nodes to incorporate patches and new features, and is in charge of a backup strategy for crucial cluster data. To help job seekers and employers have a standard means to demonstrate and evaluate proficiency in developing with a Kubernetes environment, the Cloud Native Computing Foundation (CNCF) developed the Certified Kubernetes Administrator (CKA) (*https://oreil.ly/Ds8nq*) program. To achieve this certification, you need to pass an exam.

There are two other Kubernetes certifications you can find on the CNCF web page. The Certified Kubernetes Application Developer (CKAD) (*https://oreil.ly/RxHwQ*) focuses on the developer-centric application of Kubernetes. The Certified Kubernetes Security Specialist (CKS) (*https://oreil.ly/53csH*) was created to verify the competence on security-based topics and requires a successful pass of the CKA exam before you can register. Passing the CKAD and CKS are not mandatory for taking the CKA exam.

In this study guide, I will explore the topics covered in the CKA exam to fully prepare you to pass the certification exam. We'll look at determining when and how you should apply the core concepts of Kubernetes to manage an application. We'll also examine the kubectl command-line tool, a mainstay of the Kubernetes engineer. I will also offer tips to help you better prepare for the exam and share my personal experience with getting ready for all aspects of it.

The CKA is different from the typical multiple-choice format of other certifications. It's completely performance based and requires you to demonstrate deep knowledge of the tasks at hand under immense time pressure. Are you ready to pass the test on the first go?

Who This Book Is For

The primary target group for this book is administrators who want to prepare for the CKA exam. The "exam details and resources" content covers all aspects of the exam curriculum, though basic knowledge of the Kubernetes architecture and its concepts is expected. If you are completely new to Kubernetes, I recommend reading *Kubernetes Up & Running* by Brendan Burns, Joe Beda, Kelsey Hightower, and Lachlan Evenson (O'Reilly) or *Kubernetes in Action* by Marko Lukša (Manning Publications) first.

What You Will Learn

The content of the book condenses the most important aspects relevant to the CKA exam. Cloud-provider-specific Kubernetes implementations like AKS or GKE do not need to be considered. Given the plethora of configuration options available in Kubernetes, it's almost impossible to cover all use cases and scenarios without duplicating the official documentation. Test takers are encouraged to reference the Kubernetes documentation (*https://oreil.ly/MoLjc*) as the go-to compendium for broader exposure.

The outline of the book follows the CKA curriculum to a T. While there might be a more natural, didactical structure for learning Kubernetes in general, the curriculum outline will help test takers prepare for the exam by focusing on specific topics. As a result, you will find yourself cross-referencing other chapters of the book depending on your existing knowledge level.

Be aware that this book covers only the concepts relevant to the CKA exam. Certain primitives that you may expect to be covered by the certification curriculum—for example, the API primitive Ingress—are not discussed. Refer to the Kubernetes documentation or other books if you want to dive deeper.

Practical experience with Kubernetes is key to passing the exam. Each chapter contains a section named "Sample Exercises" with practice questions. Solutions to those questions can be found in the Appendix.

Conventions Used in This Book

The following typographical conventions are used in this book:

Italic
> Indicates new terms, URLs, and email addresses.

Constant width

Used for filenames, file extensions, and program listings, as well as within paragraphs to refer to program elements such as variable or function names, databases, data types, environment variables, statements, and keywords.

Constant width bold

Shows commands or other text that should be typed literally by the user.

Constant width italic

Shows text that should be replaced with user-supplied values or by values determined by context.

 This element signifies a tip or suggestion.

 This element signifies a general note.

 This element indicates a warning or caution.

Using Code Examples

The source code for all examples and exercises in this book is available on GitHub (*https://github.com/bmuschko/cka-study-guide*). The repository is distributed under the Apache License 2.0. The code is free to use in commercial and open source projects. If you encounter an issue in the source code or if you have a question, open an issue in the GitHub issue tracker (*https://oreil.ly/09Z7p*). I'll be happy to have a conversation and fix any issues that might arise.

This book is here to help you get your job done. In general, if example code is offered with this book, you may use it in your programs and documentation. You do not need to contact us for permission unless you're reproducing a significant portion of the code. For example, writing a program that uses several chunks of code from this book does not require permission. Selling or distributing examples from O'Reilly books does require permission. Answering a question by citing this book and quoting example code does not require permission. Incorporating a significant amount of example code from this book into your product's documentation does require permission. We appreciate, but generally do not require, attribution. An attribution usually includes the title, author, publisher, and ISBN. For example: "*Certified Kubernetes Administrator (CKA) Study Guide* by Benjamin Muschko (O'Reilly). Copyright 2022 Some Benjamin Muschko, 978-1-098-10722-2."

If you feel your use of code examples falls outside fair use or the permission given above, feel free to contact us at *permissions@oreilly.com*.

O'Reilly Interactive Katacoda Labs

Interactive Katacoda scenarios mimic real-world production environments and let you write and run code as you learn, right in your browser. The author has developed a collection of Katacoda scenarios to give you hands-on practice with the tools and practices outlined in this book. Visit *http://oreilly.com* for more information about our interactive content, to view the ebook format for this title, and also to learn about all our learning platform has to offer.

O'Reilly Online Learning

 For more than 40 years, *O'Reilly Media* has provided technology and business training, knowledge, and insight to help companies succeed.

Our unique network of experts and innovators share their knowledge and expertise through books, articles, and our online learning platform. O'Reilly's online learning platform gives you on-demand access to live training courses, in-depth learning paths, interactive coding environments, and a vast collection of text and video from O'Reilly and 200+ other publishers. For more information, visit *http://oreilly.com*.

How to Contact Us

Please address comments and questions concerning this book to the publisher:

O'Reilly Media, Inc.
1005 Gravenstein Highway North
Sebastopol, CA 95472
800-998-9938 (in the United States or Canada)
707-829-0515 (international or local)
707-829-0104 (fax)

We have a web page for this book, where we list errata, examples, and any additional information. You can access this page at *https://oreil.ly/cka-study-guide*.

Email *bookquestions@oreilly.com* to comment or ask technical questions about this book.

For news and information about our books and courses, visit *http://oreilly.com*.

Find us on LinkedIn: *https://linkedin.com/company/oreilly-media*

Follow us on Twitter: *http://twitter.com/oreillymedia*

Watch us on YouTube: *http://youtube.com/oreillymedia*

Follow the author on Twitter: *https://twitter.com/bmuschko*

Follow the author on GitHub: *https://github.com/bmuschko*

Follow the author's blog: *https://bmuschko.com*

Acknowledgments

Every book project is a long journey and would not be possible without the help of the editorial staff and technical reviewers. Special thanks go to Jonathon Johnson, Kaslin Fields, and Werner Dijkerman for their detailed technical guidance and feedback. I would also like to thank the editors at O'Reilly Media, John Devins and Michele Cronin, for their continued support and encouragement.

## CHAPTER 1

Exam Details and Resources

This introduction chapter addresses the most pressing questions candidates ask when preparing for the Certified Kubernetes Administrator (CKA) (*https://oreil.ly/7G8Jm*) exam. We will discuss the target audience for the certification, the curriculum, and the exam environment, as well as tips and tricks and additional learning resources. If you're already familiar with the certification program, you can directly jump to any of the chapters covering the technical concepts.

Exam Objectives

Kubernetes clusters need to be installed, configured, and maintained by skilled professionals. That's the job of a Kubernetes administrator. The CKA certification program verifies a deep understanding of the typical administration tasks encountered on the job, more specifically Kubernetes cluster maintenance, networking, storage solutions, and troubleshooting applications and cluster nodes.

Kubernetes version used during the exam

At the time of writing, the exam is based on Kubernetes 1.23. All content in this book will follow the features, APIs, and command-line support for that specific version. It's certainly possible that future versions will break backward compatibility. While preparing for the certification, review the Kubernetes release notes (*https://oreil.ly/DUGrM*) and practice with the Kubernetes version used during the exam to avoid unpleasant surprises.

Curriculum

The following overview lists the high-level sections of the CKA and their scoring weight:

- 25%: Cluster Architecture, Installation, and Configuration
- 15%: Workloads and Scheduling
- 20%: Services and Networking
- 10%: Storage
- 30%: Troubleshooting

The CKA curriculum went through a major overhaul in September 2020 (*https://oreil.ly/WYnzL*). One of the reasons why the exam domains have been reorganized and optimized is the new Certified Kubernetes Security Specialist (CKS) certification (*https://oreil.ly/Oxpg9*). For the most part, security-related topics have been moved to the CKS, while the CKA continues to focus on typical administration activities and features.

> The outline of the book follows the CKA curriculum to a T. While there might be a more natural, didactical organization structure to learn Kubernetes in general, the curriculum outline will help test takers prepare for the exam by focusing on specific topics. As a result, you will find yourself cross-referencing other chapters of the book depending on your existing knowledge level.

Let's break down each domain in detail in the next sections.

Cluster Architecture, Installation, and Configuration

This section of the curriculum touches on all things Kubernetes cluster-related. This includes understanding the basic architecture of a Kubernetes clusters such as control plane versus worker nodes, high-availability setups, and the tooling for installing, upgrading, and maintaining a cluster. You will need to demonstrate the process of installing a cluster from scratch, upgrading a cluster version, and backing up/restoring the etcd database. The Cloud Native Computing Foundation (CNCF) also decided to add a somewhat unrelated topic to this section: managing role-based access control (RBAC). RBAC is an important concept every administrator should understand how to set up and apply.

Workloads and Scheduling

Administrators need to have a good grasp of Kubernetes concepts used for operating cloud-native applications. The section "Workloads and Scheduling" addresses this need. You need to be familiar with Deployments, ReplicaSets, and configuration data specified by ConfigMaps and Secrets. When creating a new Pod, the Kubernetes scheduler places the object on an available node. Scheduling rules like node affinity and taints/tolerations control and fine-tune the behavior. For the exam, you are only required to understand the effect of Pod resource limits on scheduling. Furthermore, you need to be familiar with imperative and declarative manifest management, as well as common templating tools like Kustomize, yq, and Helm.

Services and Networking

A cloud-native microservice rarely runs in isolation. In the majority of cases, it needs to interact with other microservices or external systems. Understanding Pod-to-Pod communication, exposing applications outside of the cluster, and configuring cluster networking is extremely important to administrators to ensure a functioning system. In this section of the exam, you need to demonstrate your knowledge of the Kubernetes primitives Service and Ingress.

Storage

This section covers the different types of volumes for reading and writing data. As an administrator, you need to know how to create and configure them. Persistent volumes ensure permanent data persistence even beyond a cluster node restart. You will need to be familiar with the mechanics and demonstrate how to mount a persistent volume to a path in a container. Make sure you understand the differences between static and dynamic binding.

Troubleshooting

Naturally, things can go south in production Kubernetes clusters. Sometimes, the application is misbehaving, becomes unresponsive, or even inaccessible. Other times, the cluster nodes may crash or run into configuration issues. It is of upmost importance to develop effective strategies for troubleshooting those situations so that they can be resolved as quickly as possible. This section of the exam has the highest scoring weight. You will be confronted with typical scenarios that you need to fix by taking appropriate measures.

Involved Kubernetes Primitives

The main purpose of the exam is to test your practical knowledge of Kubernetes primitives. It is to be expected that the exam combines multiple concepts in a single problem. Refer to Figure 1-1 as a rough guide to the applicable Kubernetes resources and their relationships.

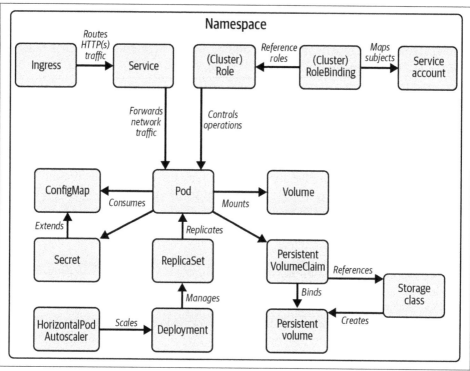

Figure 1-1. Kubernetes primitives relevant to the exam

Exam Environment and Tips

To take the CKA exam, you must purchase a voucher as registration. A voucher can be acquired on the CNCF training and certification web page (*https://oreil.ly/tkBY1*). On occasion, the CNCF offers discounts for the voucher (e.g., around the US holiday Thanksgiving). Those discount offers are often announced on the Twitter account @LF_Training (*https://oreil.ly/TDBVP*).

With the voucher in hand, you can schedule a time for the exam. On the day of your scheduled test, you'll be asked to log into the test platform with a URL provided to you by email. You'll be asked to enable the audio and video feed on your computer to discourage you from cheating. A proctor will oversee your actions via audio/video feed and terminate the session if she thinks you are not following the rules.

Exam attempts

The voucher you purchased grants two attempts to pass the CKA exam. I recommend preparing reasonably well before taking the test on the first attempt. It will give you a fair chance to pass the test and provide you with a good impression of the exam environment and the complexity of the questions. Don't sweat it if you do not pass the test on the first attempt. You've got another free shot.

The CKA has a time limit of two hours. During that time window, you'll need to solve hands-on problems on a real, predefined Kubernetes cluster. Every question will state the cluster you need to work on. Using a practical approach to gauge a candidate's skill set is superior to tests with multiple-choice questions as you can translate the knowledge directly on tasks performed on the job.

You are permitted to open an additional browser tab to navigate the official Kubernetes documentation assets. Those pages include *https://oreil.ly/w0vib*, *https://oreil.ly/XLYLj*, and *https://oreil.ly/1sr3B* plus their subdomains. You are allowed to create bookmarks and open them during the exam as long as they fall within the URLs just mentioned.

While having the Kubernetes documentation pages at hand is extremely valuable, make sure you know *where* to find the relevant information within those pages. In preparation for the test, read all the documentation pages from start to end at least one time. Don't miss out on the search functionality of the official documentation pages.

Using the documentation efficiently

Using a search term will likely lead you to the right documentation pages quicker than navigating the menu items. Copying and pasting code snippets from the documentation into the console of the exam environment works reasonably well. Sometimes you may have to adjust the YAML indentation manually as the proper formatting may get lost in the process.

I'd highly recommend reading the FAQ for the CKA exam (*https://oreil.ly/xJeV8*). You will find answers to most of your pressing questions there, including system requirements for your machine, scoring, certification renewal, and retake requirements.

Candidate Skills

The certification assumes that you already have a basic understanding of Kubernetes. You should be familiar with Kubernetes internals, its core concepts, and the command-line tool kubectl. The CNCF offers a free "Introduction to Kubernetes" course (*https://oreil.ly/U48YJ*) for beginners to Kubernetes, as well as training courses on more advanced topics.

The CKA exam assumes that you work in the role of an administrator and that you are confronted with typical maintenance tasks on a day-to-day basis. In addition to the command-line tool kubectl, you will need to be familiar with other tools relevant to operating a Kubernetes cluster. The following points lay out the tooling landscape:

Kubernetes architecture and concepts
> The exam may ask you to install a Kubernetes cluster from scratch. Read up on the basics of Kubernetes and its architectural components. Don't expect to encounter any multiple-choice questions during the exam.

The kubectl *command-line tool*
> The kubectl command-line tool is the central tool you will use during the exam to interact with the Kubernetes cluster. Even if you have only a little time to prepare for the exam, it's essential to practice how to operate kubectl, as well as its commands and their relevant options. You will have no access to the web dashboard UI (*https://oreil.ly/Fizsg*) during the exam.

Kubernetes cluster maintenance tools
> Installing a Kubernetes cluster from scratch and upgrading the Kubernetes version of an existing cluster is performed using the tool kubeadm. It's important to understand its usage and the relevant process to walk through the process. Additionally, you need to have a good understanding of the tool etcdctl including its command-line options for backing up and restoring the etcd database.

Other relevant tools
> Kubernetes objects are represented by YAML or JSON. The content of this book will only use examples in YAML, as it is more commonly used than JSON in the Kubernetes world. You will have to edit YAML during the exam to create a new object declaratively or when modifying the configuration of a live object. Ensure that you have a good handle on basic YAML syntax, data types, and indentation conforming to the specification. How do you edit the YAML definitions, you may ask? From the terminal, of course. The exam terminal environment comes with

the tools vi and vim preinstalled. Practice the keyboard shortcuts for common operations (especially how to exit the editor). The last tool I want to mention is GNU Bash. It's imperative that you understand the basic syntax and operators of the scripting language. It's absolutely possible that you may have to read, modify, or even extend a multiline Bash command running in a container. Having a good working knowledge of Linux and the shell command line is going to be helpful when interacting with cluster nodes.

Time Management

Candidates have a time limit of two hours to complete the exam. At a minimum, 66% of the answers to the questions need to be correct. Many of the questions consist of multiple steps. While the Linux Foundation doesn't provide a breakdown on the scoring, I'd assume that partially correct answers will still score a portion of the points.

When taking the test, you will notice that the given time limit will put you under a lot of pressure. That's intentional. The Linux Foundation expects Kubernetes practitioners to be able to apply their knowledge to real-world scenarios by finding solutions to problems in a timely fashion.

The CKA exam will present you with a mix of problems. Some are short and easy to solve; others require more context and take more time. Personally, I tried to tackle the easy problems first in order to score as many points as possible without getting stuck on the harder questions. I marked down any questions I could not solve immediately in the notepad functionality integrated in the exam environment. During the second pass, revisit the questions you skipped and try to solve them as well. In the optimal case, you will have been able to work through all problems in the allotted time.

Command-Line Tips and Tricks

Given that the command line is going to be your solidary interface to the Kubernetes cluster, it's essential that you become extremely familiar with the tools kubectl, kubeadm, etcdctl, and their available options. This section touches on a couple of tips and tricks for making their use more efficient and productive.

Setting a Context and Namespace

The CKA exam environment comes with six Kubernetes clusters already set up for you. Take a look at the instructions (*https://oreil.ly/SM8d6*) for a high-level, technical overview of those clusters. Each of the exam exercises needs to be solved on a designated cluster, as outlined by its description. Furthermore, the instructions will ask you to work in a namespace other than default. You will need to make sure to set the context and namespace as the first course of action before working on a question. The following command sets the context and the namespace as a one-time action:

```
$ kubectl config set-context <context-of-question> \
  --namespace=<namespace-of-question>
$ kubectl config use-context <context-of-question>
```

Using an Alias for kubectl

In the course of the exam, you will have to execute the kubectl command tens or even hundreds of times. You might be an extremely fast keyboard typer, however, there's no point in fully spelling out the executable over and over again. It is far more efficient to set an alias for the kubectl command. The following alias command maps the letter k to the full kubectl command:

```
$ alias k=kubectl
$ k version
```

You can repeat the same process for other command-line tools like kubeadm and etcdctl to save even more typing. The exam environment already sets up an alias for the kubectl command.

Using kubectl Command Auto-Completion

Memorizing kubectl commands and command-line options takes a lot of practice. During the exam, you are allowed to configure bash auto-completion. The instructions are available in the Kubernetes documentation in the section "bash auto-completion on Linux" (*https://oreil.ly/Tb6Qg*). Make sure you understand the trade-off between the time needed to set up auto-completion versus typing commands and options by hand.

Internalize Resource Short Names

Many of the kubectl commands can be quite lengthy. For example, the command for managing Persistent volume claims is persistentvolumeclaims. Having to spell out the full command can be error-prone and time-consuming. Thankfully, some of the longer commands come with a short-form usage. The command api-resources lists all available commands plus their short names:

```
$ kubectl api-resources
NAME                    SHORTNAMES  APIGROUP  NAMESPACED  KIND
...
persistentvolumeclaims  pvc                   true        PersistentVolumeClaim
...
```

Using `pvc` instead of `persistentvolumeclaims` results in a much more concise and expressive command execution, as shown here:

```
$ kubectl describe pvc my-claim
```

Deleting Kubernetes Objects

Certain situations require you to delete existing Kubernetes objects. For example, during the exam you may want to start a task from scratch with a clean slate because you made a configuration mistake, or you may want to change the runtime configuration of an object that requires the re-creation of it instead of modifying the live object. Upon execution of the `delete` command, Kubernetes tries to delete the targeted object gracefully so that there's minimal impact on the end user. If the object cannot be deleted within the default grace period (30 seconds), the kubelet attempts to forcefully kill the object.

During the CKA exam, end user impact is not a concern. The most important goal is to complete all tasks in the time frame granted to the candidate. Therefore, waiting on an object to be deleted gracefully is a waste of time. You can force an immediate deletion of an object with the command-line option with the `--force` option. The following command kills the Pod named `nginx` using a `SIGKILL` signal:

```
$ kubectl delete pod nginx --force
```

Finding Object Information

As an administrator, you are often confronted with a situation that requires you to investigate a failure situation in a Kubernetes cluster. This cluster may already run workloads that consist of a set of different object types. The CKA exam will emulate failure scenarios to test your troubleshooting skills.

Listing objects of a specific type helps identify the root cause of issues; however, you will need to ensure to search for relevant information. You can combine the `describe` and `get` commands with the Unix command `grep` to filter objects by search term. The `-C` command-line option of the `grep` command renders contextual configuration before and after the search term.

The following commands show their usage. The first command finds all Pods with the annotation key-value pair `author=John Doe` plus the surrounding 10 lines. The second command searches the YAML representation of all Pods for their labels including the surrounding five lines of output:

```
$ kubectl describe pods | grep -C 10 "author=John Doe"
$ kubectl get pods -o yaml | grep -C 5 labels:
```

Discovering Command Options

The Kubernetes documentation is extensive and covers the most important aspects of the ecosystem including the API reference for Kubernetes resources. While the search functionality drastically reduces the time for finding the relevant information by search term, you might have to further browse through the resulting pages.

An alternative route is the help functionality built into kubectl using the command-line option --help. The option renders the details of commands and subcommands including options and examples. The following command demonstrates the use of the --help option for the create command:

```
$ kubectl create --help
Create a resource from a file or from stdin.

JSON and YAML formats are accepted.

Examples:
  ...

Available Commands:
  ...

Options:
  ...
```

Moreover, you can explore available fields for every Kubernetes resource with the explain command. As a parameter, provide the JSONPath (*https://oreil.ly/34Op9*) of the object you'd like to render details for. The following example lists all fields of a Pod's spec:

```
$ kubectl explain pods.spec
KIND:     Pod
VERSION:  v1

RESOURCE: spec <Object>

DESCRIPTION:
  ...

FIELDS:
  ...
```

Practicing and Practice Exams

Hands-on practice is extremely important when it comes to passing the exam. For that purpose, you'll need a functioning Kubernetes cluster environment. The following options stand out:

- Find out if your employer already has a Kubernetes cluster set up and will allow you to use it to practice.

- For practicing the installation or upgrade process of Kubernetes cluster nodes, I found it useful to run one or many virtual machines using Vagrant (*https://oreil.ly/2jLJS*) and VirtualBox (*https://oreil.ly/3BhDj*). Those tools help with creating an isolated Kubernetes environment that is easy to bootstrap and dispose on-demand. Some of the practice exercises in this book use this setup as the starting point.

- Installing Kubernetes on your developer machine is an easy and fast way to get set up. The Kubernetes documentation provides various installation options (*https://oreil.ly/JrBUh*), depending on your operating system. Minikube is specifically useful when it comes to experimenting with more advanced features like Ingress or storage classes.

- If you're a subscriber to the O'Reilly Learning Platform (*https://oreil.ly/xOtTT*), you have unlimited access to scenarios running a Kubernetes environment in Katacoda (*https://oreil.ly/gYiVj*).

You may also want to try one of the following paid learning and practice resources:

- The book *Certified Kubernetes Application Developer (CKAD) Study Guide* (O'Reilly) covers the curriculum of the CKAD certification; however, given the overlap of topics between the CKAD and the CKA, you will find useful information in it.

- Certified Kubernetes Administrator (CKA) Cert Prep: The Basics (*https://oreil.ly/oqnRq*) is a video-based course on LinkedIn Learning that focuses exclusively on study tips.

- Killer Shell (*https://killer.sh*) is a simulator with sample exercises for all Kubernetes certifications.

- Certified Kubernetes Administrator (CKA) with Practice Tests (*https://oreil.ly/QWQFP*) offers videos on all topics relevant to the exam, as well as an integrated practice environment. You'll need to purchase a subscription to access the content, but the content is very thorough, well-explained, and hands-on.

- The CKA practice exam from Study4Exam (*https://oreil.ly/uIwU9*) offers a commercial, web-based test environment to assess your knowledge level.

Summary

The CKA exam verifies your hands-on knowledge of installing, maintaining, upgrading, and troubleshooting a Kubernetes cluster. Furthermore, you are expected to understand Kubernetes resource types typically used for running, exposing, and scaling a cloud-native application in a Kubernetes environment. The exam curriculum groups those topics into categories with different weights. You are faced with a challenging hands-on test that asks you to solve real-world problems in an actual Kubernetes environment. The Linux Foundation does not publish how solutions to particular questions are scored. It's safe to say that partial solutions will be counted, though.

In this chapter, we discussed everything you need know about the exam to get started. We touched on the exam environment, tips and tricks for time management, tools a candidate needs to be familiar with, and additional learning and practicing resources.

The following chapters align with the exam curriculum so that you can map the content to the learning objectives. At the end of each chapter, you will find sample exercises to practice your knowledge level.

## CHAPTER 2

Cluster Architecture, Installation, and Configuration

According to the name of the chapter, the first section of the curriculum refers to typical tasks you'd expect of a Kubernetes administrator. Those tasks include understanding the architectural components of a Kubernetes cluster, setting up a cluster from scratch, and maintaining a cluster going forward.

Interestingly, this section also covers the security aspects of a cluster, more specifically role-based access control (RBAC). You are expected to understand how to map permissions for operations to API resources for a set of users or processes.

At the end of this chapter, you will understand the tools and procedures for installing and maintaining a Kubernetes cluster. Moreover, you'll know how to configure RBAC for representative, real-world use cases.

At a high level, this chapter covers the following concepts:

- Understanding RBAC
- Installing of a cluster with `kubeadm`
- Upgrading a version of a Kubernetes cluster with `kubeadm`
- Backing up and restoring etcd with `etcdctl`
- Understanding a highly available Kubernetes cluster

Role-Based Access Control

In Kubernetes you need to be authenticated before you are allowed to make a request to an API resource. A cluster administrator usually has access to all resources and operations. The easiest way to operate a cluster is to provide everyone with an admin account. While "admin access for everyone" sounds fantastic as you grow your business, it comes with a considerable amount of risk. Users may accidentally delete a Secret Kubernetes object, which likely breaks one or many applications and therefore has a tremendous impact on end users. As you can imagine, this approach is not a good idea for production environments that run mission-critical applications.

As with other production systems, only certain users should have full access, whereas the majority of users have read-only access (and potentially access to mutate the system) depending on the role. For example, application developers do not need to manage cluster nodes. They only need to tend to the objects required to run and configure their application.

RBAC defines policies for users, groups, and processes by allowing or disallowing access to manage API resources. Enabling and configuring RBAC is mandatory for any organization with a strong emphasis on security. For the exam, you need to understand the involved RBAC API resource types and how to create and configure them in different scenarios.

RBAC High-Level Overview

RBAC helps with implementing a variety of use cases:

- Establishing a system for users with different roles to access a set of Kubernetes resources
- Controlling processes running in a Pod and the operations they can perform via the Kubernetes API
- Limiting the visibility of certain resources per namespace

RBAC consists of three key building blocks, as shown in Figure 2-1. Together, they connect API primitives and their allowed operations to the so-called subject, which is a user, a group, or a ServiceAccount.

The following list breaks down the responsibilities by terminology:

Subject
> The user or process that wants to access a resource

Resource
> The Kubernetes API resource type (e.g., a Deployment or node)

Verb

The operation that can be executed on the resource (e.g., creating a Pod or deleting a Service)

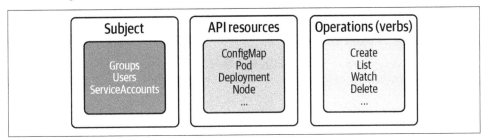

Figure 2-1. RBAC key building blocks

Creating a Subject

In the context of RBAC, you can use a user account, service account, or a group as a subject. Users and groups are not stored in etcd, the Kubernetes database, and are meant for processes running outside of the cluster. Service accounts exists as objects in Kubernetes and are used by processes running inside of the cluster. In this section, you'll learn how to create them.

User accounts and groups

Kubernetes does not represent a user as with an API resource. The user is meant to be managed by the administrator of a Kubernetes cluster, which then distributes the credentials of the account to the real person or to be used by an external process.

Calls to the API server with a user need to be authenticated. Kubernetes offers a variety of authentication methods for those API requests. Table 2-1 shows different ways of authenticating RBAC subjects.

Table 2-1. Authentication strategies for managing RBAC subjects

Authentication strategy	Description
X.509 client certificate	Uses an OpenSSL client certificate to authenticate
Basic authentication	Uses username and password to authenticate
Bearer tokens	Uses OpenID (a flavor of OAuth2) or webhooks as a way to authenticate

To keep matters simple, the following steps demonstrate the creation of a user that uses an OpenSSL client certificate to authenticate. Those actions have to be performed with the cluster-admin Role object. During the exam, you will not have to create a user yourself. You can assume that the relevant setup has been performed for you. Therefore, you will not need to memorize the following steps:

1. Log into the Kubernetes control plane node and create a temporary directory that will hold the generated keys. Navigate into the directory:

   ```
   $ mkdir cert && cd cert
   ```

2. Create a private key using the openssl executable. Provide an expressive file name, such as <username>.key:

   ```
   $ openssl genrsa -out johndoe.key 2048
   Generating RSA private key, 2048 bit long modulus
   ............................+
   ..+
   e is 65537 (0x10001)
   $ ls
   johndoe.key
   ```

3. Create a certificate sign request (CSR) in a file with the extension .csr. You need to provide the private key from the previous step. The -subj option provides the username (CN) and the group (O). The following command uses the username johndoe and the group named cka-study-guide. To avoid assigning the user to a group, leave off the /O component of the assignment:

   ```
   $ openssl req -new -key johndoe.key -out johndoe.csr -subj \
     "/CN=johndoe/O=cka-study-guide"
   $ ls
   johndoe.csr johndoe.key
   ```

4. Lastly, sign the CSR with the Kubernetes cluster certificate authority (CA). The CA can usually be found in the directory /etc/kubernetes/pki and needs to contain the files ca.crt and ca.key. We are going to use minikube here, which stores those files in the directory pass:[<code>~/.minikube</code>]. The following command signs the CSR and makes it valid for 364 days:

   ```
   $ openssl x509 -req -in johndoe.csr -CA /.minikube/ca.crt -CAkey \
     /.minikube/ca.key -CAcreateserial -out johndoe.crt -days 364
   Signature ok
   subject=/CN=johndoe/O=cka-study-guide
   Getting CA Private Key
   ```

5. Create the user in Kubernetes by setting a user entry in kubeconfig for johndoe. Point to the CRT and key file. Set a context entry in kubeconfig for johndoe:

   ```
   $ kubectl config set-credentials johndoe \
     --client-certificate=johndoe.crt --client-key=johndoe.key
   User "johndoe" set.
   $ kubectl config set-context johndoe-context --cluster=minikube \
     --user=johndoe
   Context "johndoe-context" modified.
   ```

6. To switch to the user, use the context named johndoe-context. You can check the current context using the command config current-context:

```
$ kubectl config use-context johndoe-context
Switched to context "johndoe-context".
$ kubectl config current-context
johndoe-context
```

ServiceAccount

A user represents a real person who commonly interacts with the Kubernetes cluster using the kubectl executable or the UI dashboard. Some service applications like Helm (*https://helm.sh*) running inside of a Pod need to interact with the Kubernetes cluster by making requests to the API server via RESTful HTTP calls. For example, a Helm chart would define multiple Kubernetes objects required for a business application. Kubernetes uses a ServiceAccount to authenticate the Helm service process with the API server through an authentication token. This ServiceAccount can be assigned to a Pod and mapped to RBAC rules.

A Kubernetes cluster already comes with a ServiceAccount, the default ServiceAccount that lives in the default namespace. Any Pod that doesn't explicitly assign a ServiceAccount uses the default ServiceAccount.

To create a custom ServiceAccount imperatively, run the create serviceaccount command:

```
$ kubectl create serviceaccount build-bot
serviceaccount/build-bot created
```

The declarative way to create a ServiceAccount looks very straightforward. You simply provide the appropriate kind and a name, as shown in Example 2-1.

Example 2-1. A YAML manifest defining a ServiceAccount

```
apiVersion: v1
kind: ServiceAccount
metadata:
  name: build-bot
```

Listing ServiceAccounts

Listing the ServiceAccounts can be achieved with the get serviceaccounts command. As you can see in the following output, the default namespace lists the default ServiceAccount and the custom ServiceAccount we just created:

```
$ kubectl get serviceaccounts
NAME        SECRETS   AGE
build-bot   1         78s
default     1         93d
```

Rendering ServiceAccount Details

Upon object creation, the API server creates a Secret holding the API token and assigns it to the ServiceAccount. The Secret and token names use the ServiceAccount name as a prefix. You can discover the details of a ServiceAccount using the describe serviceaccount command, as shown here:

```
$ kubectl describe serviceaccount build-bot
Name:                build-bot
Namespace:           default
Labels:              <none>
Annotations:         <none>
Image pull secrets:  <none>
Mountable secrets:   build-bot-token-rvjnz
Tokens:              build-bot-token-rvjnz
Events:              <none>
```

Consequently, you should be able to find a Secret object for the default and the build-bot ServiceAccount:

```
$ kubectl get secrets
NAME                      TYPE                                     DATA   AGE
build-bot-token-rvjnz     kubernetes.io/service-account-token      3      20m
default-token-qgh5n       kubernetes.io/service-account-token      3      93d
```

Assigning a ServiceAccount to a Pod

For a ServiceAccount to take effect, it needs to be assigned to a Pod running the application intended to make API calls. Upon Pod creation, you can use the command-line option --serviceaccount in conjunction with the run command:

```
$ kubectl run build-observer --image=alpine --restart=Never \
    --serviceaccount=build-bot
pod/build-observer created
```

Alternatively, you can directly assign the ServiceAccount in the YAML manifest of a Pod, Deployment, Job, or CronJob using the field serviceAccountName. Example 2-2 shows the definition of a ServiceAccount to a Pod.

Example 2-2. A YAML manifest assigning a ServiceAccount to a Pod

```
apiVersion: v1
kind: Pod
metadata:
  name: build-observer
spec:
  serviceAccountName: build-bot
...
```

Understanding RBAC API Primitives

With those key concepts in mind, let's take a look at the Kubernetes API primitives that implement the RBAC functionality:

Role
> The Role API primitive declares the API resources and their operations this rule should operate on. For example, you may want to say "allow listing and deleting of Pods," or you may express "allow watching the logs of Pods," or even both with the same Role. Any operation that is not spelled out explicitly is disallowed as soon as it is bound to the subject.

RoleBinding
> The RoleBinding API primitive *binds* the Role object to the subject(s). It is the glue for making the rules active. For example, you may want to say "bind the Role that permits updating Services to the user John Doe."

Figure 2-2 shows the relationship between the involved API primitives. Keep in mind that the image renders only a selected list of API resource types and operations.

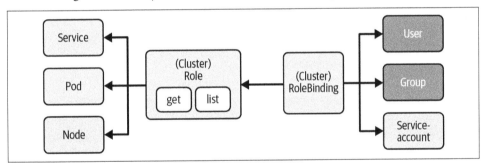

Figure 2-2. RBAC primitives

The following sections demonstrate the namespace-wide usage of Roles and Role-Bindings, but the same operations and attributes apply to cluster-wide Roles and RoleBindings, discussed in "Namespace-wide and Cluster-wide RBAC" on page 24.

Default User-Facing Roles

Kubernetes defines a set of default Roles. You can assign them to a subject via a RoleBinding or define your own, custom Roles depending on your needs. Table 2-2 describes the default user-facing Roles.

Table 2-2. Default User-Facing Roles

Default ClusterRole	Description
cluster-admin	Allows read and write access to resources across all namespaces.
admin	Allows read and write access to resources in namespace including Roles and RoleBindings.
edit	Allows read and write access to resources in namespace except Roles and RoleBindings. Provides access to Secrets.
view	Allows read-only access to resources in namespace except Roles, RoleBindings, and Secrets.

To define new Roles and RoleBindings, you will have to use a context that allows for creating or modifying them, that is, cluster-admin or admin.

Creating Roles

Roles can be created imperatively with the `create role` command. The most important options for the command are `--verb` for defining the verbs aka operations, and `--resource` for declaring a list of API resources. The following command creates a new Role for the resources Pod, Deployment, and Service with the verbs `list`, `get`, and `watch`:

```
$ kubectl create role read-only --verb=list,get,watch \
  --resource=pods,deployments,services
role.rbac.authorization.k8s.io/read-only created
```

Declaring multiple verbs and resources for a single imperative `create role` command can be declared as a comma-separated list for the corresponding command-line option or as multiple arguments. For example, `--verb=list,get,watch` and `--verb=list --verb=get --verb=watch` carry the same instructions. You may also use the wildcard "*" to refer to all verbs or resources.

The command-line option `--resource-name` spells out one or many object names that the policy rules should apply to. A name of a Pod could be `nginx` and listed here with its name. Providing a list of resource names is optional. If no names have been provided, then the provided rules apply to all objects of a resource type.

The declarative approach can become a little lengthy. As you can see in Example 2-3, the section `rules` lists the resources and verbs. Resources with an API group, like Deployments that use the API version `apps/v1`, need to explicitly declare it under the attribute `apiGroups`. All other resources (e.g., Pods and Services), simply use an empty string as their API version doesn't contain a group. Be aware that the imperative command for creating a Role automatically determines the API group.

Example 2-3. A YAML manifest defining a Role

```
apiVersion: rbac.authorization.k8s.io/v1
kind: Role
metadata:
  name: read-only
rules:
- apiGroups:
  - ""
  resources:
  - pods
  - services
  verbs:
  - list
  - get
  - watch
- apiGroups:
  - apps
  resources:
  - deployments
  verbs:
  - list
  - get
  - watch
```

Listing Roles

Once the Role has been created, its object can be listed. The list of Roles renders only the name and the creation timestamp. Each of the listed roles does not give away any of its details:

```
$ kubectl get roles
NAME        CREATED AT
read-only   2021-06-23T19:46:48Z
```

Rendering Role Details

You can inspect the details of a Role using the describe command. The output renders a table that maps a resource to its permitted verbs. This cluster has no resources created, so the list of resource names in the following console output is empty:

```
$ kubectl describe role read-only
Name:         read-only
Labels:       <none>
Annotations:  <none>
PolicyRule:
  Resources         Non-Resource URLs  Resource Names  Verbs
  ---------         -----------------  --------------  -----
  pods              []                 []              [list get watch]
```

```
services          []                    []                    [list get watch]
deployments.apps  []                    []                    [list get watch]
```

Creating RoleBindings

The imperative command creating a RoleBinding object is `create rolebinding`. To bind a Role to the RoleBinding, use the `--role` command-line option. The subject type can be assigned by declaring the options `--user`, `--group`, or `--serviceaccount`. The following command creates the RoleBinding with the name `read-only-binding` to the user called `johndoe`:

```
$ kubectl create rolebinding read-only-binding --role=read-only --user=johndoe
rolebinding.rbac.authorization.k8s.io/read-only-binding created
```

Example 2-4 shows a YAML manifest representing the RoleBinding. You can see from the structure that a role can be mapped to one or many subjects. The data type is an array indicated by the dash character under the attribute `subjects`. At this time, only the user `johndoe` has been assigned.

Example 2-4. A YAML manifest defining a RoleBinding

```
apiVersion: rbac.authorization.k8s.io/v1
kind: RoleBinding
metadata:
  name: read-only-binding
roleRef:
  apiGroup: rbac.authorization.k8s.io
  kind: Role
  name: read-only
subjects:
- apiGroup: rbac.authorization.k8s.io
  kind: User
  name: johndoe
```

Listing RoleBindings

The most important information the list of RoleBindings gives away is the associated Role. The following command shows that the RoleBinding `read-only-binding` has been mapped to the Role `read-only`:

```
$ kubectl get rolebindings
NAME               ROLE             AGE
read-only-binding  Role/read-only   24h
```

The output does not provide an indication of the subjects. You will need to render the details of the object for more information, as described in the next section.

Rendering RoleBinding Details

RoleBindings can be inspected using the describe command. The output renders a table of subjects and the assigned role. The following example renders the descriptive representation of the RoleBinding named read-only-binding:

```
$ kubectl describe rolebinding read-only-binding
Name:          read-only-binding
Labels:        <none>
Annotations:   <none>
Role:
  Kind:  Role
  Name:  read-only
Subjects:
  Kind  Name      Namespace
  ----  ----      ---------
  User  johndoe
```

Seeing the RBAC Rules in Effect

Let's see how Kubernetes enforces the RBAC rules for the scenario we set up so far. First, we'll create a new Deployment with the cluster-admin credentials. In Minikube, this user is assigned to the context minikube:

```
$ kubectl config current-context
minikube
$ kubectl create deployment myapp --image=nginx --port=80 --replicas=2
deployment.apps/myapp created
```

Now, we'll switch the context for the user johndoe:

```
$ kubectl config use-context johndoe-context
Switched to context "johndoe-context".
```

Remember that the user johndoe is permitted to list deployments. We'll verify that by using the get deployments command:

```
$ kubectl get deployments
NAME    READY   UP-TO-DATE   AVAILABLE   AGE
myapp   2/2     2            2           8s
```

The RBAC rules only allow listing Deployments, Pods, and Services. The following command tries to list the ReplicaSets, which results in an error:

```
$ kubectl get replicasets
Error from server (Forbidden): replicasets.apps is forbidden: User "johndoe" \
cannot list resource "replicasets" in API group "apps" in the namespace "default"
```

A similar behavior can be observed when trying to use other verbs than `list`, `get`, or `watch`. The following command tries to delete a Deployment:

```
$ kubectl delete deployment myapp
Error from server (Forbidden): deployments.apps "myapp" is forbidden: User \
"johndoe" cannot delete resource "deployments" in API group "apps" in the \
namespace "default"
```

At any given time, you can check a user's permissions with the `auth can-i` command. The command gives you the option to list all permissions or check a specific permission:

```
$ kubectl auth can-i --list --as johndoe
Resources              Non-Resource URLs   Resource Names   Verbs
...
pods                   []                  []               [list get watch]
services               []                  []               [list get watch]
deployments.apps       []                  []               [list get watch]
$ kubectl auth can-i list pods --as johndoe
yes
```

Namespace-wide and Cluster-wide RBAC

Roles and RoleBindings apply to a particular namespace. You will have to specify the namespace at the time of creating both objects. Sometimes, a set of Roles and Rolebindings needs to apply to multiple namespaces or even the whole cluster. For a cluster-wide definition, Kubernetes offers the API resource types ClusterRole and ClusterRoleBinding. The configuration elements are effectively the same. The only difference is the value of the `kind` attribute:

- To define a cluster-wide Role, use the imperative subcommand `clusterrole` or the kind `ClusterRole` in the YAML manifest.

- To define a cluster-wide RoleBinding, use the imperative subcommand `cluster rolebinding` or the kind `ClusterRoleBinding` in the YAML manifest.

Aggregating RBAC Rules

Existing ClusterRoles can be aggregated to avoid having to redefine a new, composed set of rules that likely leads to duplication of instructions. For example, say you wanted to combine a user-facing role with a custom Role. An aggregated ClusterRule can merge rules via label selection without having to copy-paste the existing rules into one.

Say we defined two ClusterRoles shown in Examples 2-5 and 2-6. The ClusterRole `list-pods` allows for listing Pods and the ClusterRole `delete-services` allows for deleting Services.

Example 2-5. A YAML manifest defining a ClusterRole for listing Pods

```
apiVersion: rbac.authorization.k8s.io/v1
kind: ClusterRole
metadata:
  name: list-pods
  namespace: rbac-example
  labels:
    rbac-pod-list: "true"
rules:
- apiGroups:
  - ""
  resources:
  - pods
  verbs:
  - list
```

Example 2-6. A YAML manifest defining a ClusterRole for deleting Services

```
apiVersion: rbac.authorization.k8s.io/v1
kind: ClusterRole
metadata:
  name: delete-services
  namespace: rbac-example
  labels:
    rbac-service-delete: "true"
rules:
- apiGroups:
  - ""
  resources:
  - services
  verbs:
  - delete
```

To aggregate those rules, ClusterRoles can specify an `aggregationRule`. This attribute describes the label selection rules. Example 2-7 shows an aggregated ClusterRole defined by an array of `matchLabels` criteria. The ClusterRole does not add its own rules as indicated by `rules: []`; however, there's no limiting factor that would disallow it.

Example 2-7. A YAML manifest defining a ClusterRole with aggregated rules

```
apiVersion: rbac.authorization.k8s.io/v1
kind: ClusterRole
metadata:
  name: pods-services-aggregation-rules
  namespace: rbac-example
aggregationRule:
  clusterRoleSelectors:
  - matchLabels:
```

```
        rbac-pod-list: "true"
  - matchLabels:
      rbac-service-delete: "true"
rules: []
```

We can verify the proper aggregation behavior of the ClusterRole by describing the object. You can see in the following output that both ClusterRoles, `list-pods` and `delete-services`, have been taken into account:

```
$ kubectl describe clusterroles pods-services-aggregation-rules -n rbac-example
Name:         pods-services-aggregation-rules
Labels:       <none>
Annotations:  <none>
PolicyRule:
  Resources  Non-Resource URLs  Resource Names  Verbs
  ---------  -----------------  --------------  -----
  services   []                 []              [delete]
  pods       []                 []              [list]
```

For more information on ClusterRole label selection rules, see the official documentation (*https://oreil.ly/J6k3m*). The page also explains how to aggregate the default user-facing ClusterRoles.

Creating and Managing a Kubernetes Cluster

When thinking about the typical tasks of a Kubernetes administrator, I am sure that at least one of the following bread-and-butter activities comes to mind:

- Bootstrapping a control plane node
- Bootstrapping worker nodes and joining them to the cluster
- Upgrading a cluster to a newer version

The low-level command-line tool for performing cluster bootstrapping operations is called kubeadm. It is not meant for provisioning the underlying infrastructure. That's the purpose of infrastructure automation tools like Ansible and Terraform. To install kubeadm, follow the installation instructions (*https://oreil.ly/gKq4m*) in the official Kubernetes documentation.

While not explicitly stated in the CKA frequently asked questions (FAQ) page, you can assume that the kubeadm executable has been preinstalled for you. The following sections describe the processes for creating and managing a Kubernetes cluster on a high level and will use kubeadm heavily. For more detailed information, see the step-by-step Kubernetes reference documentation I will point out for each of the tasks.

Installing a Cluster

The most basic topology of a Kubernetes cluster consists of a single node that acts as the control plane and the worker node at the same time. By default, many developer-centric Kubernetes installations like minikube or Docker Desktop start with this configuration. While a single-node cluster may be a good option for a Kubernetes playground, it is not a good foundation for scalability and high-availability reasons. At the very least, you will want to create a cluster with a single control plane and one or many nodes handling the workload.

This section explains how to install a cluster with a single control plane and one worker node. You can repeat the worker node installation process to add more worker nodes to the cluster. You can find a full description of the installation steps (*https://oreil.ly/8visY*) in the official Kubernetes documentation. Figure 2-3 illustrates the installation process.

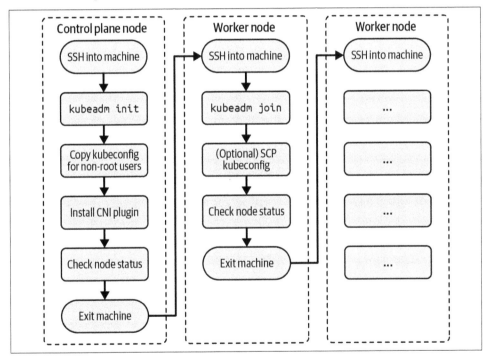

Figure 2-3. Process for a cluster installation process

Initializing the Control Plane Node

Start by initializing the control plane on the control plane node. The control plane is the machine responsible for hosting the API server, etcd, and other components important to managing the Kubernetes cluster.

Open an interactive shell to the control plane node using the ssh command. The following command targets the control plane node named kube-control-plane running Ubuntu 18.04.5 LTS:

```
$ ssh kube-control-plane
Welcome to Ubuntu 18.04.5 LTS (GNU/Linux 4.15.0-132-generic x86_64)
...
```

Initialize the control plane using the kubeadm init command. You will need to add the following two command-line options: provide the IP addresses for the Pod network with the option --pod-network-cidr. With the option --apiserver-advertise-address, you can declare the IP address the API Server will advertise to listen on.

The console output renders a kubeadm join command. Keep that command around for later. It is important for joining worker nodes to the cluster in a later step.

 Retrieving the join command for worker nodes

You can always retrieve the join command by running kubeadm token create --print-join-command on the control plane node should you lose it.

The following command uses 172.18.0.0/16 for the Classless Inter-Domain Routing (CIDR) and IP address 10.8.8.10 for the API server:

```
$ sudo kubeadm init --pod-network-cidr 172.18.0.0/16 \
  --apiserver-advertise-address 10.8.8.10
...
To start using your cluster, you need to run the following as a regular user:

  mkdir -p $HOME/.kube
  sudo cp -i /etc/kubernetes/admin.conf $HOME/.kube/config
  sudo chown $(id -u):$(id -g) $HOME/.kube/config

You should now deploy a pod network to the cluster.
Run "kubectl apply -f [podnetwork].yaml" with one of the options listed at:
  https://kubernetes.io/docs/concepts/cluster-administration/addons/

Then you can join any number of worker nodes by running the following on \
each as root:

kubeadm join 10.8.8.10:6443 --token fi8io0.dtkzsy9kws56dmsp \
  --discovery-token-ca-cert-hash \
  sha256:cc89ea1f82d5ec460e21b69476e0c052d691d0c52cce83fbd7e403559c1ebdac
```

After the init command has finished, run the necessary commands from the console output to start the cluster as nonroot user:

```
$ mkdir -p $HOME/.kube
$ sudo cp -i /etc/kubernetes/admin.conf $HOME/.kube/config
$ sudo chown $(id -u):$(id -g) $HOME/.kube/config
```

You must deploy a Container Network Interface (CNI) plugin (*https://oreil.ly/t6eJ7*) so that Pods can communicate with each other. You can pick from a wide range of networking plugins listed in the Kubernetes documentation (*https://oreil.ly/1Y7MF*). Popular plugins include Flannel, Calico, and Weave Net. Sometimes you will see the term "add-ons" in the documentation, which is synonymous with plugin.

The CKA exam will most likely ask you to install a specific add-on. Most of the installation instructions live on external web pages, not permitted to be used during the exam. Make sure that you search for the relevant instructions in the official Kubernetes documentation. For example, you can find the installation instructions for Weave Net here (*https://oreil.ly/86YpI*). The following command installs the Weave Net objects:

```
$ kubectl apply -f "https://cloud.weave.works/k8s/net?k8s-version= \
  $(kubectl version | base64 | tr -d '\n')"
serviceaccount/weave-net created
clusterrole.rbac.authorization.k8s.io/weave-net created
clusterrolebinding.rbac.authorization.k8s.io/weave-net created
role.rbac.authorization.k8s.io/weave-net created
rolebinding.rbac.authorization.k8s.io/weave-net created
daemonset.apps/weave-net created
```

Verify that the control plane node indicates the "Ready" status using the command `kubectl get nodes`. It might take a couple of seconds before the node transitions from the "NotReady" status to the "Ready" status. You have an issue with your node installation in case the status transition does not occur. Refer to Chapter 7 for debugging strategies:

```
$ kubectl get nodes
NAME                STATUS   ROLES                  AGE    VERSION
kube-control-plane  Ready    control-plane,master   24m    v1.21.2
```

Exit the control plane node using the `exit` command:

```
$ exit
logout
...
```

Joining the Worker Nodes

Worker nodes are responsible for handling the workload scheduled by the control plane. Examples of workloads are Pods, Deployments, Jobs, and CronJobs. To add a worker node to the cluster so that it can be used, you will have to run a couple of commands, as described next.

Open an interactive shell to the worker node using the `ssh` command. The following command targets the worker node named `kube-worker-1` running Ubuntu 18.04.5 LTS:

```
$ ssh kube-worker-1
Welcome to Ubuntu 18.04.5 LTS (GNU/Linux 4.15.0-132-generic x86_64)
...
```

Run the `kubeadm join` command provided by the `kubeadm init` console output on the control plane node. The following command shows an example. Remember that the token and SHA256 hash will be different for you:

```
$ sudo kubeadm join 10.8.8.10:6443 --token fi8io0.dtkzsy9kws56dmsp \
  --discovery-token-ca-cert-hash \
  sha256:cc89ea1f82d5ec460e21b69476e0c052d691d0c52cce83fbd7e403559c1ebdac
[preflight] Running pre-flight checks
[preflight] Reading configuration from the cluster...
[preflight] FYI: You can look at this config file with \
'kubectl -n kube-system get cm kubeadm-config -o yaml'
[kubelet-start] Writing kubelet configuration to file \
"/var/lib/kubelet/config.yaml"
[kubelet-start] Writing kubelet environment file with \
flags to file "/var/lib/kubelet/kubeadm-flags.env"
[kubelet-start] Starting the kubelet
[kubelet-start] Waiting for the kubelet to perform the TLS Bootstrap...

This node has joined the cluster:
* Certificate signing request was sent to apiserver and a response was received.
* The Kubelet was informed of the new secure connection details.

Run 'kubectl get nodes' on the control plane to see this node join the cluster.
```

You won't be able to run the `kubectl get nodes` command from the worker node without copying the administrator kubeconfig file from the control plane node. Follow the instructions (*https://oreil.ly/AIM8a*) in the Kubernetes documentation to do so or log back into the control plane node. Here, we are just going to log back into the control plane node. You should see that the worker node has joined the cluster and is in a "Ready" status:

```
$ ssh kube-control-plane
Welcome to Ubuntu 18.04.5 LTS (GNU/Linux 4.15.0-132-generic x86_64)
...
$ kubectl get nodes
NAME                 STATUS   ROLES                  AGE     VERSION
kube-control-plane   Ready    control-plane,master   5h49m   v1.21.2
kube-worker-1        Ready    <none>                 15m     v1.21.2
```

You can repeat the process for any other worker node you want to add to the cluster.

Managing a Highly Available Cluster

Single control plane clusters are easy to install; however, they present an issue when the node is lost. Once the control plane node becomes unavailable, any ReplicaSet running on a worker node cannot re-create a Pod due to the inability to talk back to the scheduler running on a control plane node. Moreover, clusters cannot be accessed externally anymore (e.g., via kubectl), as the API server cannot be reached.

High-availability (HA) clusters help with scalability and redundancy. For the exam, you will need to have a basic understanding about configuring them and their implications. Given the complexity of standing up an HA cluster, it's unlikely that you'll be asked to perform the steps during the exam. For a full discussion on setting up HA clusters, see the relevant page (*https://oreil.ly/17ZDL*) in the Kubernetes documentation.

The *stacked etcd topology* involves creating two or more control plane nodes where etcd is colocated on the node. Figure 2-4 shows a representation of the topology with three control plane nodes.

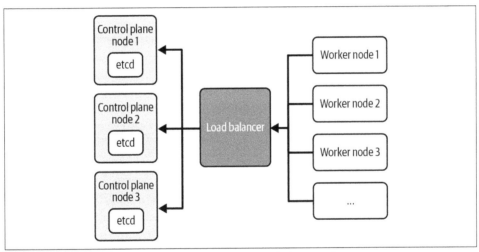

Figure 2-4. Stacked etcd topology with three control plane nodes

Each of the control plane nodes hosts the API server, the scheduler, and the controller manager. Worker nodes communicate with the API server through a load balancer. It is recommended to operate this cluster topology with a minimum of three control plane nodes for redundancy reasons due to the tight coupling of etcd to the control plane node. By default, kubeadm will create an etcd instance when joining a control plane node to the cluster.

The *external etcd node* topology separates etcd from the control plane node by running it on a dedicated machine. Figure 2-5 shows a setup with three control plane nodes, each of which run etcd on a different machine.

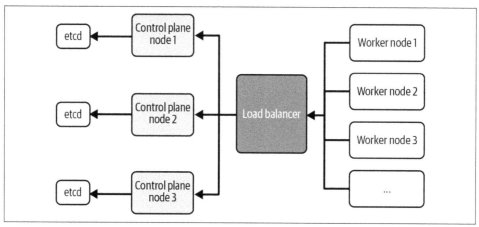

Figure 2-5. External etcd node topology

Similar to the stacked etcd topology, each control plane node hosts the API server, the scheduler, and the controller manager. The worker nodes communicate with them through a load balancer. The main difference here is that the etcd instances run on a separate host. This topology decouples etcd from other control plane functionality and therefore has less of an impact on redundancy when a control plane node is lost. As you can see in the illustration, this topology requires twice as many hosts as the stacked etcd topology.

Upgrading a Cluster Version

Over time, you will want to upgrade the Kubernetes version of an existing cluster to pick up bug fixes and new features. The upgrade process has to be performed in a controlled manner to avoid the disruption of workload currently in execution and to prevent the corruption of cluster nodes.

It is recommended to upgrade from a minor version to a next higher one (e.g., from 1.18.0 to 1.19.0), or from a patch version to a higher one (e.g., from 1.18.0 to 1.18.3). Abstain from jumping up multiple minor versions to avoid unexpected side effects. You can find a full description of the upgrade steps (*https://oreil.ly/2dCfk*) in the official Kubernetes documentation. Figure 2-6 illustrates the upgrade process.

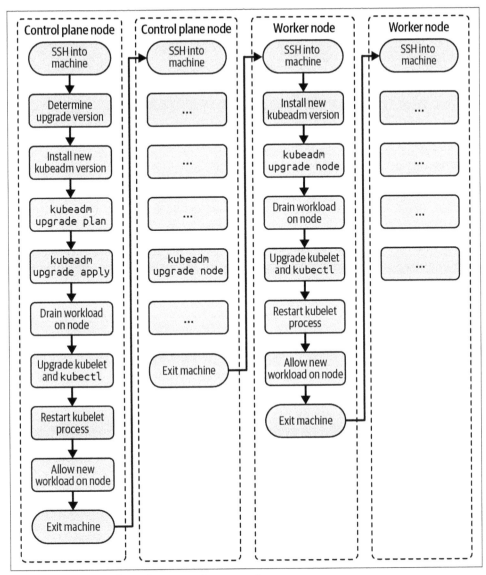

Figure 2-6. Process for a cluster version upgrade

Upgrading control plane nodes

As explained earlier, a Kubernetes cluster may employ one or many control plane nodes to better support high-availability and scalability concerns. When upgrading a cluster version, this change needs to happen for control plane nodes one at a time.

Pick one of the control plane nodes that contains the kubeconfig file (located at /etc/kubernetes/admin.conf), and open an interactive shell to the control plane node using the ssh command. The following command targets the control plane node named kube-control-plane running Ubuntu 18.04.5 LTS:

```
$ ssh kube-control-plane
Welcome to Ubuntu 18.04.5 LTS (GNU/Linux 4.15.0-132-generic x86_64)
...
```

First, check the nodes and their Kubernetes versions. In this setup, all nodes run on version 1.18.0. We are dealing with only a single control plane node and a single worker node:

```
$ kubectl get nodes
NAME                 STATUS   ROLES    AGE     VERSION
kube-control-plane   Ready    master   4m54s   v1.18.0
kube-worker-1        Ready    <none>   3m18s   v1.18.0
```

Start by upgrading the kubeadm version. Identify the version you'd like to upgrade to. On Ubuntu machines, you can use the following apt-get command. The version format usually includes a patch version (e.g., 1.20.7-00). Check the Kubernetes documentation if your machine is running a different operating system:

```
$ sudo apt update
...
$ sudo apt-cache madison kubeadm
    kubeadm |  1.21.2-00 | http://apt.kubernetes.io kubernetes-xenial/main \
    amd64 Packages
    kubeadm |  1.21.1-00 | http://apt.kubernetes.io kubernetes-xenial/main \
    amd64 Packages
    kubeadm |  1.21.0-00 | http://apt.kubernetes.io kubernetes-xenial/main \
    amd64 Packages
    kubeadm |  1.20.8-00 | http://apt.kubernetes.io kubernetes-xenial/main \
    amd64 Packages
    kubeadm |  1.20.7-00 | http://apt.kubernetes.io kubernetes-xenial/main \
    amd64 Packages
    kubeadm |  1.20.6-00 | http://apt.kubernetes.io kubernetes-xenial/main \
    amd64 Packages
    kubeadm |  1.20.5-00 | http://apt.kubernetes.io kubernetes-xenial/main \
    amd64 Packages
    kubeadm |  1.20.4-00 | http://apt.kubernetes.io kubernetes-xenial/main \
    amd64 Packages
    kubeadm |  1.20.2-00 | http://apt.kubernetes.io kubernetes-xenial/main \
    amd64 Packages
    kubeadm |  1.20.1-00 | http://apt.kubernetes.io kubernetes-xenial/main \
    amd64 Packages
    kubeadm |  1.20.0-00 | http://apt.kubernetes.io kubernetes-xenial/main \
    amd64 Packages
    ...
```

Upgrade kubeadm to a target version. Say you'd want to upgrade to version 1.19.0-00. The following series of commands installs kubeadm with that specific version and checks the currently installed version to verify:

```
$ sudo apt-mark unhold kubeadm && sudo apt-get update && sudo apt-get install \
   -y kubeadm=1.19.0-00 && sudo apt-mark hold kubeadm
Canceled hold on kubeadm.
...
Unpacking kubeadm (1.19.0-00) over (1.18.0-00) ...
Setting up kubeadm (1.19.0-00) ...
kubeadm set on hold.
$ sudo apt-get update && sudo apt-get install -y --allow-change-held-packages \
   kubeadm=1.19.0-00
...
kubeadm is already the newest version (1.19.0-00).
0 upgraded, 0 newly installed, 0 to remove and 7 not upgraded.
$ kubeadm version
kubeadm version: &version.Info{Major:"1", Minor:"19", GitVersion:"v1.19.0", \
GitCommit:"e19964183377d0ec2052d1f1fa930c4d7575bd50", GitTreeState:"clean", \
BuildDate:"2020-08-26T14:28:32Z", GoVersion:"go1.15", Compiler:"gc", \
Platform:"linux/amd64"}
```

Check which versions are available to upgrade to and validate whether your current cluster is upgradable. You can see in the output of the following command that we could upgrade to version 1.19.12. For now, we'll stick with 1.19.0:

```
$ sudo kubeadm upgrade plan
...
[upgrade] Fetching available versions to upgrade to
[upgrade/versions] Cluster version: v1.18.20
[upgrade/versions] kubeadm version: v1.19.0
I0708 17:32:53.037895    17430 version.go:252] remote version is much newer: \
v1.21.2; falling back to: stable-1.19
[upgrade/versions] Latest stable version: v1.19.12
[upgrade/versions] Latest version in the v1.18 series: v1.18.20
...
You can now apply the upgrade by executing the following command:

        kubeadm upgrade apply v1.19.12

Note: Before you can perform this upgrade, you have to update kubeadm to v1.19.12.
...
```

As described in the console output, we'll start the upgrade for the control plane. The process may take a couple of minutes. You may have to upgrade the CNI plugin as well. Follow the provider instructions for more information:

```
$ sudo kubeadm upgrade apply v1.19.0
...
[upgrade/version] You have chosen to change the cluster version to "v1.19.0"
[upgrade/versions] Cluster version: v1.18.20
[upgrade/versions] kubeadm version: v1.19.0
...
[upgrade/successful] SUCCESS! Your cluster was upgraded to "v1.19.0". Enjoy!

[upgrade/kubelet] Now that your control plane is upgraded, please proceed \
with upgrading your kubelets if you haven't already done so.
```

Drain the control plane node by evicting the workload. Any new workload won't be schedulable on the node until uncordoned:

```
$ kubectl drain kube-control-plane --ignore-daemonsets
node/kube-control-plane cordoned
WARNING: ignoring DaemonSet-managed Pods: kube-system/calico-node-qndb9, \
kube-system/kube-proxy-vpvms
evicting pod kube-system/calico-kube-controllers-65f8bc95db-krp72
evicting pod kube-system/coredns-f9fd979d6-2brkq
pod/calico-kube-controllers-65f8bc95db-krp72 evicted
pod/coredns-f9fd979d6-2brkq evicted
node/kube-control-plane evicted
```

Upgrade the kubelet and the kubectl tool to the same version:

```
$ sudo apt-mark unhold kubelet kubectl && sudo apt-get update && sudo \
  apt-get install -y kubelet=1.19.0-00 kubectl=1.19.0-00 && sudo apt-mark \
  hold kubelet kubectl
...
Setting up kubelet (1.19.0-00) ...
Setting up kubectl (1.19.0-00) ...
kubelet set on hold.
kubectl set on hold.
```

Restart the kubelet process:

```
$ sudo systemctl daemon-reload
$ sudo systemctl restart kubelet
```

Reenable the control plane node back so that the new workload can become schedulable:

```
$ kubectl uncordon kube-control-plane
node/kube-control-plane uncordoned
```

The control plane nodes should now show the usage of Kubernetes 1.19.0:

```
$ kubectl get nodes
NAME                 STATUS   ROLES    AGE   VERSION
kube-control-plane   Ready    master   21h   v1.19.0
kube-worker-1        Ready    <none>   21h   v1.18.0
```

Exit the control plane node using the exit command:

```
$ exit
logout
...
```

Upgrading worker nodes

Pick one of the worker nodes, and open an interactive shell to the node using the ssh command. The following command targets the worker node named kube-worker-1 running Ubuntu 18.04.5 LTS:

```
$ ssh kube-worker-1
Welcome to Ubuntu 18.04.5 LTS (GNU/Linux 4.15.0-132-generic x86_64)
...
```

Upgrade kubeadm to a target version. This is the same command you used for the control plane node, as explained earlier:

```
$ sudo apt-mark unhold kubeadm && sudo apt-get update && sudo apt-get install \
  -y kubeadm=1.19.0-00 && sudo apt-mark hold kubeadm
Canceled hold on kubeadm.
...
Unpacking kubeadm (1.19.0-00) over (1.18.0-00) ...
Setting up kubeadm (1.19.0-00) ...
kubeadm set on hold.
$ kubeadm version
kubeadm version: &version.Info{Major:"1", Minor:"19", GitVersion:"v1.19.0", \
GitCommit:"e19964183377d0ec2052d1f1fa930c4d7575bd50", GitTreeState:"clean", \
BuildDate:"2020-08-26T14:28:32Z", GoVersion:"go1.15", Compiler:"gc", \
Platform:"linux/amd64"}
```

Upgrade the kubelet configuration:

```
$ sudo kubeadm upgrade node
[upgrade] Reading configuration from the cluster...
[upgrade] FYI: You can look at this config file with 'kubectl -n kube-system \
get cm kubeadm-config -o yaml'
[preflight] Running pre-flight checks
[preflight] Skipping prepull. Not a control plane node.
[upgrade] Skipping phase. Not a control plane node.
[kubelet-start] Writing kubelet configuration to file \
"/var/lib/kubelet/config.yaml"
[upgrade] The configuration for this node was successfully updated!
[upgrade] Now you should go ahead and upgrade the kubelet package using your \
package manager.
```

Drain the worker node by evicting the workload. Any new workload won't be schedulable on the node until uncordoned:

```
$ kubectl drain kube-worker-1 --ignore-daemonsets
node/kube-worker-1 cordoned
WARNING: ignoring DaemonSet-managed Pods: kube-system/calico-node-2hrxg, \
kube-system/kube-proxy-qf6nl
evicting pod kube-system/calico-kube-controllers-65f8bc95db-kggbr
evicting pod kube-system/coredns-f9fd979d6-7zm4q
evicting pod kube-system/coredns-f9fd979d6-tlmhq
pod/calico-kube-controllers-65f8bc95db-kggbr evicted
pod/coredns-f9fd979d6-7zm4q evicted
pod/coredns-f9fd979d6-tlmhq evicted
node/kube-worker-1 evicted
```

Upgrade the kubelet and the kubectl tool with the same command used for the control plane node:

```
$ sudo apt-mark unhold kubelet kubectl && sudo apt-get update && sudo apt-get \
install -y kubelet=1.19.0-00 kubectl=1.19.0-00 && sudo apt-mark hold kubelet \
kubectl
...
Setting up kubelet (1.19.0-00) ...
Setting up kubectl (1.19.0-00) ...
kubelet set on hold.
kubectl set on hold.
```

Restart the kubelet process:

```
$ sudo systemctl daemon-reload
$ sudo systemctl restart kubelet
```

Reenable the worker node so that the new workload can become schedulable:

```
$ kubectl uncordon kube-worker-1
node/kube-worker-1 uncordoned
```

Listing the nodes should now show version 1.19.0 for the worker node. You won't
be able to run kubectl get nodes from the worker node without copying the
administrator kubeconfig file from the control plane node. Follow the instructions
(*https://oreil.ly/NGHaQ*) in the Kubernetes documentation to do so or log back into
the control plane node:

```
$ kubectl get nodes
NAME                STATUS   ROLES    AGE   VERSION
kube-control-plane  Ready    master   24h   v1.19.0
kube-worker-1       Ready    <none>   24h   v1.19.0
```

Exit the worker node using the exit command:

```
$ exit
logout
...
```

Backing Up and Restoring etcd

Kubernetes stores both the declared and observed states of the cluster in the distributed etcd key-value store. It's important to have a backup plan in place that can
help you with restoring the data in case of data corruption. Backing up the data
should happen periodically in short time frames to avoid losing as little historical data
as possible.

The backup process stores the ectd data in a so-called snapshot file. This snapshot file
can be used to restore the etcd data at any given time. You can encrypt the snapshot
file to protect sensitive information. The tool etcdctl is central to the backup and
restore procedure.

As an administrator, you will need to understand how to use the tool for both
operations. You may need to install etcdctl if it is not available on the control plane

node yet. You can find installation instructions (*https://oreil.ly/CrI28*) in the etcd GitHub repository. Figure 2-7 visualizes the etcd backup and restoration process.

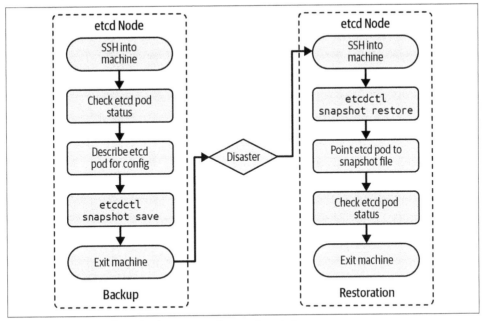

Figure 2-7. Process for a backing up and restoring etcd

Depending on your cluster topology, your cluster may consist of one or many etcd instances. Refer to the section "High-Availability Cluster Setup" for more information on how to set it up. The following sections explain a single-node etcd cluster setup. You can find additional instructions (*https://oreil.ly/PvS5u*) on the backup and restoration process for multinode etcd clusters in the official Kubernetes documentation.

Backing Up etcd

Open an interactive shell to the machine hosting etcd using the `ssh` command. The following command targets the control plane node named `kube-control-plane` running Ubuntu 18.04.5 LTS:

```
$ ssh kube-control-plane
Welcome to Ubuntu 18.04.5 LTS (GNU/Linux 4.15.0-132-generic x86_64)
...
```

Check the installed version of `etcdctl` to verify that the tool has been installed. On this node, the version is 3.4.14:

```
$ etcdctl version
etcdctl version: 3.4.14
API version: 3.4
```

Etcd is deployed as a Pod in the kube-system namespace. Inspect the version by describing the Pod. In the following output, you will find that the version is 3.4.13-0:

```
$ kubectl get pods -n kube-system
NAME                                      READY   STATUS    RESTARTS   AGE
...
etcd-kube-control-plane                   1/1     Running   0          33m
...
$ kubectl describe pod etcd-kube-control-plane -n kube-system
...
Containers:
  etcd:
    Container ID:  docker://28325c63233edaa94e16691e8082e8d86f5e7da58c0fb54 \
    d95d68dec6e80cf54
    Image:         k8s.gcr.io/etcd:3.4.3-0
    Image ID:      docker-pullable://k8s.gcr.io/etcd@sha256:4afb99b4690b418 \
    ffc2ceb67e1a17376457e441c1f09ab55447f0aaf992fa646
...
```

The same describe command reveals the configuration of the etcd service. Look for the value of the option --listen-client-urls for the endpoint URL. In the following output, the host is localhost, and the port is 2379. The server certificate is located at /etc/kubernetes/pki/etcd/server.crt defined by the option --cert-file. The CA certificate can be found at /etc/kubernetes/pki/etcd/ca.crt specified by the option --trusted-ca-file:

```
$ kubectl describe pod etcd-kube-control-plane -n kube-system
...
Containers:
  etcd:
    ...
    Command:
      etcd
      ...
      --cert-file=/etc/kubernetes/pki/etcd/server.crt
      --key-file=/etc/kubernetes/pki/etcd/server.key
      --listen-client-urls=/etc/kubernetes/pki/etcd/server.key
      --trusted-ca-file=/etc/kubernetes/pki/etcd/ca.crt
...
```

Use the etcdctl command to create the backup with version 3 of the tool. For a good starting point, copy the command from the official Kubernetes documentation (*https://oreil.ly/LuM2P*). Provide the mandatory command-line options --cacert, --cert, and --key. The option --endpoints is not needed as we are running the command on the same server as etcd. After running the command, the file /tmp/etcd-backup.db has been created:

```
$ sudo ETCDCTL_API=3 etcdctl --cacert=/etc/kubernetes/pki/etcd/ca.crt \
  --cert=/etc/kubernetes/pki/etcd/server.crt \
  --key=/etc/kubernetes/pki/etcd/server.key \
```

```
snapshot save /opt/etcd-backup.db
{"level":"info","ts":1625860312.3468597, \
"caller":"snapshot/v3_snapshot.go:119", \
"msg":"created temporary db file","path":"/opt/etcd-backup.db.part"}
{"level":"info","ts":"2021-07-09T19:51:52.356Z", \
"caller":"clientv3/maintenance.go:200", \
"msg":"opened snapshot stream; downloading"}
{"level":"info","ts":1625860312.358686, \
"caller":"snapshot/v3_snapshot.go:127", \
"msg":"fetching snapshot","endpoint":"127.0.0.1:2379"}
{"level":"info","ts":"2021-07-09T19:51:52.389Z", \
"caller":"clientv3/maintenance.go:208", \
"msg":"completed snapshot read; closing"}
{"level":"info","ts":1625860312.392891, \
"caller":"snapshot/v3_snapshot.go:142", \
"msg":"fetched snapshot","endpoint":"127.0.0.1:2379", \
"size":"2.3 MB","took":0.045987318}
{"level":"info","ts":1625860312.3930364, \
"caller":"snapshot/v3_snapshot.go:152", \
"msg":"saved","path":"/opt/etcd-backup.db"}
Snapshot saved at /opt/etcd-backup.db
```

Exit the node using the exit command:

```
$ exit
logout
...
```

Restoring etcd

You created a backup of etcd and stored it in a safe space. There's nothing else to do at this time. Effectively, it's your insurance policy that becomes relevant when disaster strikes. In the case of a disaster scenario, the data in etcd gets corrupted or the machine managing etcd experiences a physical storage failure. That's the time when you want to pull out the etcd backup for restoration.

To restore etcd from the backup, use the etcdctl snapshot restore command. At a minimum, provide the --data-dir command-line option. Here, we are using the data directory /tmp/from-backup. After running the command, you should be able to find the restored backup in the directory /var/lib/from-backup:

```
$ sudo ETCDCTL_API=3 etcdctl --data-dir=/var/lib/from-backup snapshot restore \
  /opt/etcd-backup.db
{"level":"info","ts":1625861500.5752304, \
"caller":"snapshot/v3_snapshot.go:296", \
"msg":"restoring snapshot","path":"/opt/etcd-backup.db", \
"wal-dir":"/var/lib/from-backup/member/wal", \
"data-dir":"/var/lib/from-backup", \
"snap-dir":"/var/lib/from-backup/member/snap"}
{"level":"info","ts":1625861500.6146874, \
"caller":"membership/cluster.go:392", \
```

```
"msg":"added member","cluster-id":"cdf818194e3a8c32", \
"local-member-id":"0", \
"added-peer-id":"8e9e05c52164694d", \
"added-peer-peer-urls":["http://localhost:2380"]}
{"level":"info","ts":1625861500.6350253, \
"caller":"snapshot/v3_snapshot.go:309", \
"msg":"restored snapshot","path":"/opt/etcd-backup.db", \
"wal-dir":"/var/lib/from-backup/member/wal", \
"data-dir":"/var/lib/from-backup", \
"snap-dir":"/var/lib/from-backup/member/snap"}
$ sudo ls /var/lib/from-backup
member
```

Edit the YAML manifest of the etcd Pod, which can be found at /etc/kuber
netes/manifests/etcd.yaml. Change the value of the attribute spec.volumes.host
Path with the name etcd-data from the original value /var/lib/etcd to /var/lib/
from-backup:

```
$ cd /etc/kubernetes/manifests/
$ sudo vim etcd.yaml
...
spec:
  volumes:
  ...
  - hostPath:
      path: /var/lib/from-backup
      type: DirectoryOrCreate
    name: etcd-data
...
```

The etcd-kube-control-plane Pod will be re-created, and it points to the restored
backup directory:

```
$ kubectl get pod etcd-kube-control-plane -n kube-system
NAME                       READY   STATUS    RESTARTS   AGE
etcd-kube-control-plane    1/1     Running   0          5m1s
```

In case the Pod doesn't transition into the "Running" status, try to delete it manually with the command kubectl delete pod etcd-kube-control-plane -n kube-
system.

Exit the node using the exit command:

```
$ exit
logout
...
```

Summary

Production-ready Kubernetes clusters should employ security policies to control
which users and what processes can manage objects. Role-based access control

(RBAC) defines those rules. RBAC introduces specific API resources that map subjects to the operations allowed for particular objects. Rules can be defined on a namespace or cluster level using the API resource types Role, ClusterRole, RoleBinding, and ClusterRoleBinding. To avoid duplication of rules, ClusterRoles can be aggregated with the help of label selection.

As a Kubernetes administrator, you need to be familiar with typical tasks involving the management of the cluster nodes. The primary tool for installing new nodes and upgrading a node version is kubeadm. The cluster topology of such a cluster can vary. For optimal results with redundancy and scalability, consider configuring the cluster with a high-availability setup that uses three or more control plane nodes and dedicated etcd hosts.

Backing up the etcd database should be performed as a periodic process to prevent the loss of crucial data in the event of a node or storage corruption. You can use the tool etcdctl to back up and restore etcd from the control plane node or via an API endpoint.

Exam Essentials

Know how to define RBAC rules
Defining RBAC rules involves a couple of moving parts: the subject defined by users, groups, and ServiceAccounts; the RBAC-specific API resources on the namespace and cluster level; and, finally, the verbs that allow the corresponding operations on the Kubernetes objects. Practice the creation of subjects, and how to tie them together to form the desired access rules. Ensure that you verify the correct behavior with different constellations.

Know how to create and manage a Kubernetes cluster
Installing new cluster nodes and upgrading the version of an existing cluster node are typical tasks performed by a Kubernetes administrator. You do not need to memorize all the steps involved. The documentation provides a step-by-step, easy-to-follow manual for those operations. For upgrading a cluster version, it is recommended to jump up by a single minor version or multiple patch versions before tackling the next higher version. High-availability clusters help with redundancy and scalability. For the exam, you will need to understand the different HA topologies though it's unlikely that you'll have to configure one of them as the process would involve a suite of different hosts.

Practice backing up and restoring etcd
The process for etcd disaster recovery is not as well documented as you'd expect. Practice the backup and a restoration process hands-on a couple of times to get the hang of it. Remember to point the control plane node(s) to the restored snapshot file to recover the data.

Sample Exercises

Solutions to these exercises are available in the Appendix.

1. Create the ServiceAccount named `api-access` in a new namespace called `apps`.

2. Create a ClusterRole with the name `api-clusterrole`, and create a ClusterRoleBinding named `api-clusterrolebinding`. Map the ServiceAccount from the previous step to the API resources `pods` with the operations `watch`, `list`, and `get`.

3. Create a Pod named `operator` with the image `nginx:1.21.1` in the namespace `apps`. Expose the container port 80. Assign the ServiceAccount `api-access` to the Pod. Create another Pod named `disposable` with the image `nginx:1.21.1` in the namespace `rm`. Do not assign the ServiceAccount to the Pod.

4. Open an interactive shell to the Pod named `operator`. Use the command-line tool `curl` to make an API call to list the Pods in the namespace `rm`. What response do you expect? Use the command-line tool `curl` to make an API call to delete the Pod `disposable` in the namespace `rm`. Does the response differ from the first call? You can find information about how to interact with Pods using the API via HTTP in the reference guide (*https://oreil.ly/SZls9*).

5. Navigate to the directory *app-a/ch02/upgrade-version* of the checked-out GitHub repository *bmuschko/cka-study-guide* (*https://oreil.ly/jUIq8*). Start up the VMs running the cluster using the command `vagrant up`. Upgrade all nodes of the cluster from Kubernetes 1.20.4 to 1.21.2. The cluster consists of a single control plane node named `k8s-control-plane`, and three worker nodes named `worker-1`, `worker-2`, and `worker-3`. Once done, shut down the cluster using `vagrant destroy -f`.

   Prerequisite: This exercise requires the installation of the tools Vagrant (*https://oreil.ly/sasln*) and VirtualBox (*https://oreil.ly/9Cvg9*).

6. Navigate to the directory *app-a/ch02/backup-restore-etcd* of the checked-out GitHub repository *bmuschko/cka-study-guide* (*https://oreil.ly/jUIq8*). Start up the VMs running the cluster using the command `vagrant up`. The cluster consists of a single control plane node named `k8s-control-plane` and two worker nodes named `worker-1` and `worker-2`. The `etcdctl` tool has been preinstalled on the node `k8s-control-plane`. Back up etcd to the snapshot file `/opt/etcd.bak`. Restore etcd from the snapshot file. Use the data directory `/var/bak`. Once done, shut down the cluster using `vagrant destroy -f`.

   Prerequisite: This exercise requires the installation of the tools Vagrant (*https://oreil.ly/sasln*) and VirtualBox (*https://oreil.ly/9Cvg9*).

## CHAPTER 3

Workloads

When we talk about workloads in Kubernetes (*https://oreil.ly/Uz1gG*), we mean the API resource types that run an application. Those API resource types include a Deployment, ReplicaSet, StatefulSet, DaemonSet, Job, CronJob, and of course the Pod. The curriculum of the CKA is very specific about the types of workload you need to be familiar with. The exam will include only the Deployment, ReplicaSet, and Pod. You will need to understand replication and rollout features managed by a Deployment and understand the API primitives for injecting configuration data into a Pod.

This chapter will use the concept of a volume. Take a look through Chapter 6 for more information if you're not familiar with Kubernetes' persistent storage options.

At a high level, this chapter covers the following concepts:

- A basic understanding of Deployments
- Deployment rollout and rollback functionality
- Manual and automatic scaling of the replicas controlled by a ReplicaSet
- ConfigMap and Secret

Managing Workloads with Deployments

In Kubernetes, a workload is executed in a Pod. There are various API resources that manage one or many Pods. In this section, we'll concentrate on the API resources

Deployment and ReplicaSet, which are most relevant to the exam. Moreover, we'll briefly touch on the StatefulSet, which manages workloads that hold state.

Understanding Deployments

The central API resource for running an application in a container is the Pod. Using a single instance of a Pod to operate an application has its flaws. It represents a single point of failure as all traffic targeting the application is funneled to this Pod. This behavior is specifically problematic when the load increases due to higher demand (e.g., during peak shopping season for an e-commerce application or when a central microservice like an authentication provider is used by an increasing number of other microservices within the system). Another important aspect of running an application in a Pod is failure tolerance. A Pod will not be rescheduled in the case of a node failure and therefore can lead to a system outage for end users. In this section, we'll talk about the Kubernetes mechanics that support aspects such as application scalability and failure tolerance.

A *ReplicaSet* is a Kubernetes API resource that controls multiple, identical instances of a Pod running the application, so-called replicas. It has the capability of scaling the number of replicas up or down on demand. Moreover, it knows how to roll out a new version of the application across all replicas.

A *Deployment* abstracts the functionality of ReplicaSet and manages it internally. In practice, this means that you do not have to create, modify, or delete ReplicaSet objects yourself. The Deployment keeps a history of application versions and can roll back to an older version to counteract a blocking or potentially costly production issue. Furthermore, it offers the capability of scaling the number of replicas.

Figure 3-1 illustrates the relationship between a Deployment, a ReplicaSet, and its controlled replicas.

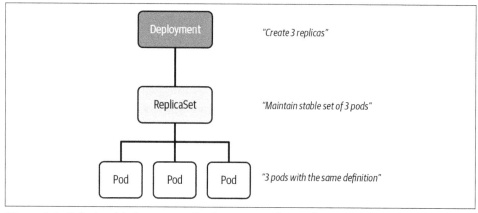

Figure 3-1. Relationship between a Deployment and a ReplicaSet

The following sections will explain how to manage Deployments, including scaling and rollout features.

Creating Deployments

You can create a Deployment using the imperative command `create deployment`. The command offers a range of options, some of which are mandatory. At a minimum, you need to provide the name of the Deployment and the container image that should be used by the replicas. The default number of replicas created is 1; however, you can define a higher number of replicas using the option `--replicas`.

Let's see the command in action. The following command creates the Deployment named `app-cache`, which runs the object cache Memcached (*https://memcached.org*) inside of the container on four replicas:

```
$ kubectl create deployment app-cache --image=memcached:1.6.8 --replicas=4
deployment.apps/app-cache created
```

The mapping between the Deployment and the replicas it controls happens through label selection. When you run the imperative command, `kubectl` already sets up the mapping for you. Example 3-1 shows the label selection in the YAML manifest. This YAML manifest can be used to create a Deployment declaratively or by inspecting the live object created by the previous imperative command.

Example 3-1. A YAML manifest for a Deployment

```
apiVersion: apps/v1
kind: Deployment
metadata:
  name: app-cache
  labels:
    app: app-cache
spec:
  replicas: 4
  selector:
    matchLabels:
      app: app-cache
  template:
    metadata:
      labels:
        app: app-cache
    spec:
      containers:
      - name: memcached
        image: memcached:1.6.8
```

When created by the imperative command, `app` is the label key the Deployment uses by default. You can find this key in three different places in the YAML output:

1. `metadata.labels`
2. `spec.selector.matchLabels`
3. `spec.template.metadata.labels`

For label selection to work properly, the assignment of `spec.selector.matchLabels` and `spec.template.metadata` needs to match, as shown in Figure 3-2.

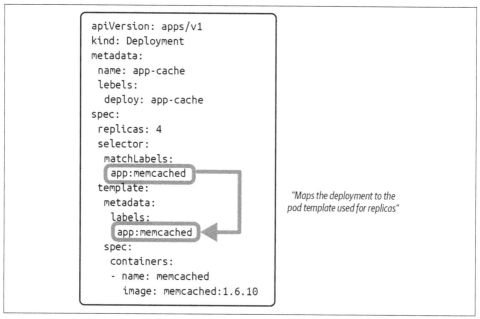

Figure 3-2. Deployment label selection

The values of `metadata.labels` is irrelevant for mapping the Deployment to the Pod template. As you can see in Figure 3-2, the label assignment to `metadata.labels` has been changed deliberately to `deploy: app-cache` to underline that it is not important for the Deployment to Pod template selection.

Listing Deployments and Their Pods

You can inspect a Deployment after its creation by using the `get deployments` command. The output of the command renders the important details of its replicas, as shown here:

```
$ kubectl get deployments
NAME        READY   UP-TO-DATE   AVAILABLE   AGE
app-cache   4/4     4            4           125m
```

You can observe the following column titles relevant to the replicas controlled by the Deployment in Table 3-1.

Table 3-1. Runtime replica information when listing deployments

Column Title	Description
READY	Lists the number of replicas available to end users in the format of <ready>/<desired>. The number of desired replicas corresponds to the value of `spec.replicas`.
UP-TO-DATE	Lists the number of replicas that have been updated to achieve the desired state.
AVAILABLE	Lists the number of replicas available to end users.

The Pods controlled by the Deployment can be identified by the naming prefix in their names. In the case of the previously created Deployment, the Pods' names start with `app-cache-`. The hash following the prefix is autogenerated and assigned to the name upon creation:

```
$ kubectl get pods
NAME                          READY   STATUS    RESTARTS   AGE
app-cache-596bc5586d-84dkv    1/1     Running   0          6h5m
app-cache-596bc5586d-8bzfs    1/1     Running   0          6h5m
app-cache-596bc5586d-rc257    1/1     Running   0          6h5m
app-cache-596bc5586d-tvm4d    1/1     Running   0          6h5m
```

Rendering Deployment Details

You can render the details of a Deployment. Those details include the label selection criteria that can be extremely valuable when troubleshooting a misconfigured Deployment. The following output provides the full gist:

```
$ kubectl describe deployment app-cache
Name:                   app-cache
Namespace:              default
CreationTimestamp:      Sat, 07 Aug 2021 09:44:18 -0600
Labels:                 app=app-cache
Annotations:            deployment.kubernetes.io/revision: 1
Selector:               app=app-cache
Replicas:               4 desired | 4 updated | 4 total | 4 available | \
                        0 unavailable
StrategyType:           RollingUpdate
MinReadySeconds:        0
RollingUpdateStrategy:  25% max unavailable, 25% max surge
Pod Template:
  Labels:  app=app-cache
  Containers:
   memcached:
    Image:          memcached:1.6.10
```

```
    Port:          <none>
    Host Port:     <none>
    Environment:   <none>
    Mounts:        <none>
  Volumes:         <none>
Conditions:
  Type           Status  Reason
  ----           ------  ------
  Progressing    True    NewReplicaSetAvailable
  Available      True    MinimumReplicasAvailable
OldReplicaSets:  <none>
NewReplicaSet:   app-cache-596bc5586d (4/4 replicas created)
Events:          <none>
```

You might have noticed that the output contains a reference to a ReplicaSet. The purpose of a ReplicaSet is to *replicate* a set of identical Pods. You do not need to deeply understand the core functionality of a ReplicaSet for the exam. Just be aware that the ReplicaSet is automatically created by a Deployment and uses the Deployment's name as a prefix for the ReplicaSet similar to the Pods it controls. In the case of the previous Deployment named app-cache, the name of the ReplicaSet is app-cache-596bc5586d.

Deleting a Deployment

A Deployment takes full charge of the creation and deletion of the objects it controls, Pods and ReplicaSets. When you delete a Deployment, the corresponding objects are deleted as well. Say you are dealing with the following set of objects shown in the output:

```
$ kubectl get deployments,pods,replicasets
NAME                         READY   UP-TO-DATE   AVAILABLE   AGE
deployment.apps/app-cache    4/4     4            4           6h47m

NAME                                  READY   STATUS    RESTARTS   AGE
pod/app-cache-596bc5586d-84dkv        1/1     Running   0          6h47m
pod/app-cache-596bc5586d-8bzfs        1/1     Running   0          6h47m
pod/app-cache-596bc5586d-rc257        1/1     Running   0          6h47m
pod/app-cache-596bc5586d-tvm4d        1/1     Running   0          6h47m

NAME                                      DESIRED   CURRENT   READY   AGE
replicaset.apps/app-cache-596bc5586d      4         4         4       6h47m
```

Run the delete deployment command for a cascading deletion of its managed objects:

```
$ kubectl delete deployment app-cache
deployment.apps "app-cache" deleted
$ kubectl get deployments,pods,replicasets
No resources found in default namespace.
```

Performing Rolling Updates and Rollbacks

Rollout and rollback capabilities are built into certain API resources. Once the definition of the Pod template in a Deployment has been changed, Kubernetes knows how to apply the change to all Pods managed by the object. In this section, we'll talk about both scenarios: deploying a new version of an application and reverting to an old version of an application.

Rolling Out a New Revision

Deployments make it very easy to roll out a new version of the application to all replicas it controls. Say you want to upgrade the version of Memcached from 1.6.8 to 1.6.10 to benefit from the latest features and bug fixes. All you need to do is to change the desired state of the object by updating the Pod template. The Deployment takes care of updating all replicas to the new version one by one. This process is called a *rolling update*.

At any time, you can modify the live object using the command `edit deployment`. Alternatively, the command `set image` offers a quick and convenient way to change the image of a Deployment, as shown in the following command:

```
$ kubectl set image deployment app-cache memcached=memcached:1.6.10 --record
deployment.apps/app-cache image updated
```

The flag `--record` is optional and defaults to the value `false`. If provided without a value or set to the value `true`, the command used for the change will be recorded. Internally, the `set image` command preserves the change cause by assigning the annotation with the key `kubernetes.io/change-cause` to the Deployment.

You can check the current status of a rollout while in progress. The command to use is `rollout status`. The output gives you an indication of the number of replicas that have already been updated since emitting the command:

```
$ kubectl rollout status deployment app-cache
Waiting for rollout to finish: 2 out of 4 new replicas have been updated...
deployment "app-cache" successfully rolled out
```

Kubernetes keeps track of the changes you make to a Deployment over time in the rollout history. Every change is represented by a so-called *revision*. You can check the rollout history by running the following command. You will see two revisions listed:

```
$ kubectl rollout history deployment app-cache
deployment.apps/app-cache
REVISION   CHANGE-CAUSE
1          <none>
2          kubectl set image deployment app-cache memcached=memcached:1.6.10 \
           --record=true
```

The first revision was recorded for the original state of the Deployment when you created the object. The second revision was added for changing the image tag. Note that the column "CHANGE-CAUSE" renders the command used for the change.

To get a more detailed view on the revision, run the following command. You can see that the image uses the value memcached:1.6.10:

```
$ kubectl rollout history deployments app-cache --revision=2
deployment.apps/app-cache with revision #2
Pod Template:
  Labels:       app=app-cache
        pod-template-hash=596bc5586d
  Annotations:  kubernetes.io/change-cause: kubectl set image deployment \
                app-cache memcached=memcached:1.6.10 --record=true
  Containers:
   memcached:
    Image:        memcached:1.6.10
    Port:         <none>
    Host Port:    <none>
    Environment:        <none>
    Mounts:       <none>
  Volumes:        <none>
```

Rolling Back to a Previous Revision

Problems may arise in production that require swift action. For example, say that the container image that you just rolled out contains a crucial bug. Kubernetes gives you the option to roll back to one of the previous revisions in the rollout history. You can achieve this by using the rollout undo command. To pick a specific revision, provide the command-line option --to-revision. The command rolls back to the previous revision if you do not provide the option. Here, we are rolling back to revision 1:

```
$ kubectl rollout undo deployment app-cache --to-revision=1
deployment.apps/app-cache rolled back
```

As a result, Kubernetes performs a rolling update to all replicas with the revision 1. Checking the rollout history now lists revision 3. Given that we rolled back to revision 1, there's no more need to keep that entry as a duplicate. Kubernetes simply turns revision 1 into 3 and removes 1 from the list:

```
$ kubectl rollout history deployment app-cache
deployment.apps/app-cache
REVISION   CHANGE-CAUSE
2          kubectl set image deployment app-cache memcached=memcached:1.6.10 \
           --record=true
3          <none>
```

Scaling Workloads

Scalability is one of Kubernetes' built-in capabilities. We'll learn how to manually scale the number of replicas as a reaction to increased load on the application. Furthermore, we'll talk about the API resource Horizontal Pod Autoscaler, which allows to automatically scale the managed set of Pods based on resource thresholds like CPU and memory.

Manually Scaling a Deployment

Scaling the number of replicas controlled by a Deployment up or down is a straight-forward process. You can either manually edit the live object using `edit deployment` and change the value of the attribute `spec.replicas` or use the imperative `scale deployment` command. The following command increases the number of replicas from four to six:

```
$ kubectl scale deployment app-cache --replicas=6
deployment.apps/app-cache scaled
```

You can observe the creation of replicas in real time. If you are fast enough, you might still see the change of status for the newly created Pods turning from `Contain erCreating` to `Running`:

```
$ kubectl get pods
NAME                       READY   STATUS             RESTARTS   AGE
app-cache-5d6748d8b9-6cc4j  1/1     ContainerCreating  0          11s
app-cache-5d6748d8b9-6rmlj  1/1     Running            0          28m
app-cache-5d6748d8b9-6z7g5  1/1     ContainerCreating  0          11s
app-cache-5d6748d8b9-96dzf  1/1     Running            0          28m
app-cache-5d6748d8b9-jkjsv  1/1     Running            0          28m
app-cache-5d6748d8b9-svrxw  1/1     Running            0          28m
$ kubectl get pods
NAME                       READY   STATUS    RESTARTS   AGE
app-cache-5d6748d8b9-6cc4j  1/1     Running   0          3m17s
app-cache-5d6748d8b9-6rmlj  1/1     Running   0          32m
app-cache-5d6748d8b9-6z7g5  1/1     Running   0          3m17s
app-cache-5d6748d8b9-96dzf  1/1     Running   0          32m
app-cache-5d6748d8b9-jkjsv  1/1     Running   0          31m
app-cache-5d6748d8b9-svrxw  1/1     Running   0          32m
```

Manually scaling the number of replicas takes a little bit of guesswork. You will still have to monitor the load on your system to see if your number of replicas is sufficient to handle the incoming traffic.

Manually Scaling a StatefulSet

Another API resource that can be scaled manually is the StatefulSet. StatefulSets are meant for managing stateful applications by a set of Pods (e.g., databases). Similar to a Deployment, the StatefulSet defines a Pod template; however, each of its replicas guarantees a unique and persistent identity. Similar to a Deployment, a StatefulSet uses a ReplicaSet to manage the replicas.

We are not going to discuss StatefulSets in more detail, but you can read more about them in the documentation (*https://oreil.ly/dXJhh*). The reason we are discussing the StatefulSet API resource here is that it can be manually scaled in a similar fashion as the Deployment.

Let's say we'd deal with the YAML definition for a StatefulSet and a Service that run and expose a Redis database, as illustrated in Example 3-2.

Example 3-2. A YAML manifest for a StatefulSet and Service

```
apiVersion: v1
kind: Service
metadata:
  name: redis
  namespace: default
  labels:
    app: redis
spec:
  ports:
  - port: 6379
    protocol: TCP
  selector:
    app: redis
  type: ClusterIP
  clusterIP: None
---
apiVersion: apps/v1
kind: StatefulSet
metadata:
  name: redis
spec:
  selector:
    matchLabels:
      app: redis
  replicas: 1
  serviceName: "redis"
  template:
    metadata:
      labels:
        app: redis
    spec:
      containers:
```

```
  - name: redis
    image: redis:6.2.5
    command: ["redis-server", "--appendonly", "yes"]
    ports:
    - containerPort: 6379
      name: web
    volumeMounts:
    - name: redis-vol
      mountPath: /data
volumeClaimTemplates:
- metadata:
    name: redis-vol
  spec:
    accessModes: ["ReadWriteOnce"]
    resources:
      requests:
        storage: 1Gi
```

After its creation, listing the StatefulSet shows the number of replicas in the "READY" column. As you can see in the following output, we set the number of replicas to 1:

```
$ kubectl create -f redis.yaml
service/redis created
statefulset.apps/redis created
$ kubectl get statefulset redis
NAME    READY   AGE
redis   1/1     2m10s
$ kubectl get pods
NAME       READY   STATUS    RESTARTS   AGE
redis-0    1/1     Running   0          2m
```

The scale command we explored in the context of a Deployment works here as well. In the following command, we scale the number of replicas from one to three:

```
$ kubectl scale statefulset redis --replicas=3
statefulset.apps/redis scaled
$ kubectl get statefulset redis
NAME    READY   AGE
redis   3/3     3m43s
$ kubectl get pods
NAME       READY   STATUS    RESTARTS   AGE
redis-0    1/1     Running   0          101m
redis-1    1/1     Running   0          97m
redis-2    1/1     Running   0          97m
```

It's important to mention that the process for scaling down a StatefulSet requires all replicas to be in a healthy state. Any long-term, unresolved issues in Pods controlled by a StatefulSet can lead to a situation that can result in the application becoming unavailable to end users.

Autoscaling a Deployment

Another way to scale a Deployment is with the help of a Horizontal Pod Autoscaler (HPA). The HPA is an API primitive that defines rules for automatically scaling the number of replicas under certain conditions. The only currently supported scaling condition in the stable API version of an HPA is CPU utilization. At runtime, the HPA checks the metrics collected by the metrics server (*https://oreil.ly/Lmamb*) to determine if the average maximum CPU usage across all replicas of a Deployment is less than or greater than the defined threshold. Figure 3-3 shows a high-level architecture diagram involving an HPA.

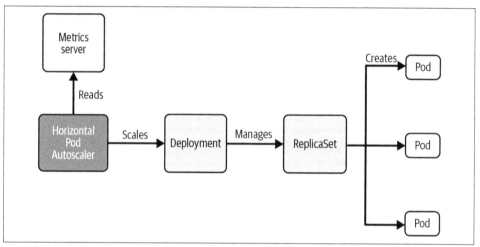

Figure 3-3. Autoscaling a Deployment

Creating Horizontal Pod Autoscalers

You can use the `autoscale deployment` command to create an HPA for an existing Deployment. The option `--cpu-percent` defines the average maximum CPU usage threshold. The options `--min` and `--max` provide the minimum number of replicas to scale down to and the maximum number of replicas the HPA can create to handle the increased load, respectively:

```
$ kubectl autoscale deployment app-cache --cpu-percent=80 --min=3 --max=5
horizontalpodautoscaler.autoscaling/app-cache autoscaled
```

The previous command is a great shortcut for creating an HPA for a Deployment. The YAML manifest representation of the HPA object looks like Example 3-3.

Example 3-3. A YAML manifest for an HPA

```
apiVersion: autoscaling/v1
kind: HorizontalPodAutoscaler
metadata:
  name: app-cache
spec:
  maxReplicas: 5
  minReplicas: 3
  scaleTargetRef:
    apiVersion: apps/v1
    kind: Deployment
    name: app-cache
  targetCPUUtilizationPercentage: 80
```

Listing Horizontal Pod Autoscalers

The short-form command for a Horizontal Pod Autoscaler is hpa. Listing all of the HPA objects transparently describes their current state: the usage of CPU utilization and the number of replicas at this time:

```
$ kubectl get hpa
NAME          REFERENCE             TARGETS          MINPODS   MAXPODS   REPLICAS \
  AGE
app-cache     Deployment/app-cache  <unknown>/80%    3         5         4        \
  58s
```

If the Pod template of the Deployment does not define CPU resource requirements or if the CPU metrics cannot be retrieved from the metrics server, the left value of the column "TARGETS" says <unknown>. Example 3-4 sets the resource requirements for the Pod template so that the HPA can work properly.

Example 3-4. Setting CPU resource requirements for Pod template

```
# ...
spec:
  # ...
  template:
    # ...
    spec:
      containers:
      - name: memcached
        # ...
        resources:
          requests:
            cpu: 250m
          limits:
            cpu: 500m
```

Once traffic hits the replicas, the current CPU usage is reflected in a percentage as shown in the following output. Here the average maximum CPU utilization is 15%:

```
$ kubectl get hpa
NAME        REFERENCE              TARGETS   MINPODS   MAXPODS   REPLICAS   AGE
app-cache   Deployment/app-cache   15%/80%   3         5         4          58s
```

Rendering Horizontal Pod Autoscaler Details

The event log of a HPA can provide additional insight into the rescaling activities. Rendering the HPA details can be a great tool for overseeing when the number of replicas was scaled up or down, as well as their scaling conditions:

```
$ kubectl describe hpa app-cache
Name:                                                    app-cache
Namespace:                                               default
Labels:                                                  <none>
Annotations:                                             <none>
CreationTimestamp:                                       Sun, 15 Aug 2021 \
                                                         15:54:11 -0600
Reference:                                               Deployment/app-cache
Metrics:                                                 ( current / target )
  resource cpu on pods  (as a percentage of request):   0% (1m) / 80%
Min replicas:                                            3
Max replicas:                                            5
Deployment pods:                                         3 current / 3 desired
Conditions:
  Type            Status   Reason            Message
  ----            ------   ------            -------
  AbleToScale     True     ReadyForNewScale  recommended size matches current size
  ScalingActive   True     ValidMetricFound  the HPA was able to successfully \
  calculate a replica count from cpu resource utilization (percentage of request)
  ScalingLimited  True     TooFewReplicas    the desired replica count is less \
  than the minimum replica count
Events:
  Type    Reason            Age    From                    Message
  ----    ------            ----   ----                    -------
  Normal  SuccessfulRescale  13m   horizontal-pod-autoscaler  New size: 3; \
  reason: All metrics below target
```

Using the Beta API Version of an Horizontal Pod Autoscaler

Kubernetes 1.12 introduced the beta API version `autoscaling/v2beta2` for a HPA, which became a final API named `autoscaling/v2` with Kubernetes 1.23. The YAML manifest of the API resource models observed metrics in a more generic way. As you can see in Example 3-5, we are inspecting CPU and memory utilization to determine if the replicas of a Deployment need to be scaled up or down.

Example 3-5. A YAML manifest for a HPA using v2

```
apiVersion: autoscaling/v2
kind: HorizontalPodAutoscaler
metadata:
  name: app-cache
spec:
  scaleTargetRef:
    apiVersion: apps/v1
    kind: Deployment
    name: app-cache
  minReplicas: 3
  maxReplicas: 5
  metrics:
  - type: Resource
    resource:
      name: cpu
      target:
        type: Utilization
        averageUtilization: 80
  - type: Resource
    resource:
      name: memory
      target:
        type: AverageValue
        averageValue: 500Mi
```

To ensure that the HPA determines the currently used resources, we'll set the memory resource requirements for the Pod template as well, as shown in Example 3-6.

Example 3-6. Setting memory resource requirements for Pod template

```
...
spec:
  ...
  template:
    ...
    spec:
      containers:
      - name: memcached
        ...
        resources:
          requests:
            cpu: 250m
            memory: 100Mi
          limits:
            cpu: 500m
            memory: 500Mi
```

Listing the HPA renders both metrics in the "TARGETS" column, as in the output of the `get` command shown here:

```
$ kubectl get hpa
NAME          REFERENCE              TARGETS               MINPODS   MAXPODS \
   REPLICAS   AGE
app-cache     Deployment/app-cache   1994752/500Mi, 0%/80%    3         5       \
   3          2m14s
```

Defining and Consuming Configuration Data

It's common to encounter an application that evaluates environment variables to control its runtime behavior. For example, the application may define an environment variable that points to the URL of an external service, or it could inject an API key used to authenticate with another microservice.

Declaring environment variables for a container is easy. You simply list them as key-value pairs under the attribute `spec.containers[].env[]`. Example 3-7 defines the environment variables `MEMCACHED_CONNECTIONS` and `MEMCACHED_THREADS` for the container named `memcached`.

Example 3-7. Environment variables set for a container

```
apiVersion: v1
kind: Pod
metadata:
  name: memcached
spec:
  containers:
  - name: memcached
    image: memcached:1.6.8
    env:
    - name: MEMCACHED_CONNECTIONS
      value: "2048"
    - name: MEMCACHED_THREADS
      value: "150"
```

If those environment variables become a common commodity across multiple Pod manifests within the same namespace, there's no way around copy-pasting the definition. For that particular use case, Kubernetes introduced the concept of configuration data represented by dedicated API resources.

Those API resources are called ConfigMap and Secret. Both define a set of key-values pairs and can be injected into a container as environment variables or mounted as a volume. Figure 3-4 illustrates the options.

Values of a Secret are only encoded

Secrets expect the value of each entry to be Base64-encoded. Base64 encodes only a value, but it doesn't encrypt it. Therefore, anyone with access to its value can decode it without problems. A Secret is distributed only to the nodes running Pods that actually require access to it. Moreover, Secrets are stored in memory and are never written to physical storage.

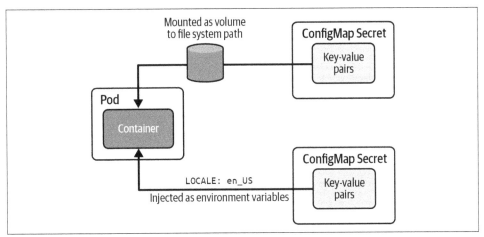

Figure 3-4. Configuration data in Kubernetes

Creating a ConfigMap

You can create a ConfigMap by emitting the imperative `create configmap` command. This command requires you to provide the source of the data as an option. Kubernetes distinguishes the four different options shown in Table 3-2.

Table 3-2. Source options for data parsed by a ConfigMap

Option	Example	Description
`--from-literal`	`--from-literal=locale=en_US`	Literal values, which are key-value pairs as plain text
`--from-env-file`	`--from-env-file=config.env`	A file that contains key-value pairs and expects them to be environment variables
`--from-file`	`--from-file=app-config.json`	A file with arbitrary contents
`--from-file`	`--from-file=config-dir`	A directory with one or many files

It's easy to confuse the options `--from-env-file` and `--from-file`. The option `--from-env-file` expects a file that contains environment variables in the format `KEY=value` separated by a new line. The key-value pairs follow typical naming conventions for environment variables (e.g., the key is uppercased, and individual words are separated by an underscore character). Historically, this option has been used to process Docker Compose .env file (*https://oreil.ly/Sd85f*), though you can use it for any other file containing environment variables. This option does not enforce or normalize the typical naming conventions for environment variables. The option - - from-file points to a file or directory containing *any* arbitrary content. It's an appropriate option for files with structured configuration data to be read by an application (e.g., a properties file, a JSON file, or an XML file).

The following command shows the creation of a ConfigMap in action. We are simply providing the key-value pairs as literals:

```
$ kubectl create configmap db-config --from-literal=DB_HOST=mysql-service \
  --from-literal=DB_USER=backend
configmap/db-config created
```

The resulting YAML object looks like the one shown in Example 3-8. As you can see, the object defines the key-value pairs in a section named data. A ConfigMap does not have a spec section.

Example 3-8. ConfigMap YAML manifest

```
apiVersion: v1
kind: ConfigMap
metadata:
  name: db-config
data:
  DB_HOST: mysql-service
  DB_USER: backend
```

Consuming a ConfigMap as Environment Variables

With the ConfigMap created, you can now inject its key-value pairs as environment variables into a container. Example 3-9 shows the use of spec.containers[].env From[].configMapRef to reference the ConfigMap by name.

Example 3-9. Injecting ConfigMap key-value pairs into the container

```
apiVersion: v1
kind: Pod
metadata:
  name: backend
spec:
  containers:
  - image: bmuschko/web-app:1.0.1
    name: backend
    envFrom:
```

```
  - configMapRef:
      name: db-config
```

After creating the Pod from the YAML manifest, you can inspect the environment variables available in the container by running the env Unix command:

```
$ kubectl exec backend -- env
...
DB_HOST=mysql-service
DB_USER=backend
...
```

Mounting a ConfigMap as a Volume

Another way to configure applications at runtime is by processing a machine-readable configuration file. Say we have decided to store the database configuration in a JSON file named db.json with the structure shown in Example 3-10.

Example 3-10. A JSON file used for configuring database information

```
{
    "db": {
      "host": "mysql-service",
      "user": "backend"
    }
}
```

Given that we are not dealing with literal key-value pairs, we need to provide the option --from-file when creating the ConfigMap object:

```
$ kubectl create configmap db-config --from-file=db.json
configmap/db-config created
```

The Pod mounts the ConfigMap as a volume to a specific path inside of the container. The assumption is that the application will read the configuration file when starting up. Example 3-11 demonstrates the YAML definition.

Example 3-11. Mounting a ConfigMap as a volume

```
apiVersion: v1
kind: Pod
metadata:
  name: backend
spec:
  containers:
  - image: bmuschko/web-app:1.0.1
    name: backend
    volumeMounts:
    - name: db-config-volume
      mountPath: /etc/config
```

```
    volumes:
    - name: db-config-volume
      configMap:
        name: db-config
```

To verify the correct behavior, open an interactive shell to the container. As you can see in the following commands, the directory /etc/config contains a file with the key we used in the ConfigMap. The content represents the JSON configuration:

```
$ kubectl exec -it backend -- /bin/sh
# ls -1 /etc/config
db.json
# cat /etc/config/db.json
{
    "db": {
      "host": "mysql-service",
      "user": "backend"
    }
}
```

Creating a Secret

You can create a Secret with the imperative command `create secret`. In addition, a mandatory subcommand needs to be provided that determines the type of the Secret. Table 3-3 lists the different types.

Table 3-3. Options for creating a Secret

Option	Description
generic	Creates a secret from a file, directory, or literal value.
docker-registry	Creates a secret for use with a Docker registry.
tls	Creates a TLS secret.

The most commonly used Secret type is `generic`. The options for a generic Secret are exactly the same as for a ConfigMap, as shown in Table 3-4.

Table 3-4. Source options for data parsed by a Secret

Option	Example	Description
--from-literal	--from-literal=password=secret	Literal values, which are key-value pairs as plain text
--from-env-file	--from-env-file=config.env	A file that contains key-value pairs and expects them to be environment variables
--from-file	--from-file=id_rsa=~/.ssh/id_rsa	A file with arbitrary contents
--from-file	--from-file=config-dir	A directory with one or many files

To demonstrate the functionality, let's create a Secret of type `generic`. The command sources the key-value pairs from the literals provided as a command-line option:

```
$ kubectl create secret generic db-creds --from-literal=pwd=s3cre!
secret/db-creds created
```

When created using the imperative command, a Secret will automatically Base64-encode the provided value. This can be observed by taking a look at the produced YAML manifest. You can see in Example 3-12 that the value `s3cre!` has been turned into `czNjcmUh`, the Base64-encoded equivalent.

Example 3-12. A Secret with Base64-encoded values

```
apiVersion: v1
kind: Secret
metadata:
  name: db-creds
type: Opaque
data:
  pwd: czNjcmUh
```

If you start with the YAML manifest to create the Secret object, you will need to create the Base64-encoded value yourself. A Unix tool that does the job is `base64`. The following command achieves exactly that:

```
$ echo -n 's3cre!' | base64
czNjcmUh
```

Alternatively, you can also use one of the specialized Secret types (*https://oreil.ly/e1Cfz*) to avoid having to provide a Base64-encoded value. The type `kubernetes.io/basic-auth` is meant for basic authentication and expects the keys `username` and `password`. The created object from this definition automatically Base64-encodes the values for both keys. Example 3-13 illustrates a YAML manifest for a Secret with type `kubernetes.io/basic-auth`. Notice that the attribute defining the key-value pairs is called `stringData` instead of `data` as used by the `Opaque` Secret type.

Example 3-13. Usage of the Secret type kubernetes.io/basic-auth

```
apiVersion: v1
kind: Secret
metadata:
  name: secret-basic-auth
type: kubernetes.io/basic-auth
stringData:
  username: bmuschko
  password: secret
```

Consuming a Secret as Environment Variables

Consuming a Secret as environment variable works similar to the way you'd do it for ConfigMaps. Here, you'd use the YAML expression `spec.containers[].env From[].secretRef` to reference the name of the Secret. Example 3-14 injects the Secret named `secret-basic-auth` as environment variables into the container named backend.

Example 3-14. Injecting Secret key-value pairs into the container

```
apiVersion: v1
kind: Pod
metadata:
  name: backend
spec:
  containers:
  - image: bmuschko/web-app:1.0.1
    name: backend
    envFrom:
    - secretRef:
        name: secret-basic-auth
```

Inspecting the environment variables in the container reveals that the Secret values do not have to be decoded. That's something Kubernetes does automatically. Therefore, the running application doesn't need to implement custom logic to decode the value. Note that Kubernetes does not verify nor normalize the typical naming conventions of environment variables, as you can see in the following output:

```
$ kubectl exec backend -- env
...
username: bmuschko
password: secret
...
```

Mounting a Secret as a Volume

To demonstrate mounting a Secret as a volume, we'll create a new Secret of type `kubernetes.io/ssh-auth`. This Secret type captures the value of an SSH private key that you can view using the command `cat ~/.ssh/id_rsa`. To process the SSH private key file with the `create secret` command, it needs to be available as a file with the name `ssh-privatekey`:

```
$ cp ~/.ssh/id_rsa ssh-privatekey
$ kubectl create secret generic secret-ssh-auth --from-file=ssh-privatekey \
  --type=kubernetes.io/ssh-auth
secret/secret-ssh-auth created
```

Mounting the Secret as a volume follows the two-step approach: define the volume first and then reference it as a mount path for one or many containers. The volume type is called `secret` as used in Example 3-15.

Example 3-15. Mounting a Secret as a volume

```
apiVersion: v1
kind: Pod
metadata:
  name: backend
spec:
  containers:
  - image: bmuschko/web-app:1.0.1
    name: backend
    volumeMounts:
    - name: ssh-volume
      mountPath: /var/app
      readOnly: true
  volumes:
  - name: ssh-volume
    secret:
      secretName: secret-ssh-auth
```

You will find the file named `ssh-privatekey` in the mount path `/var/app`. To verify, open an interactive shell and render the file contents. The contents of the file are not Base64-encoded:

```
$ kubectl exec -it backend -- /bin/sh
# ls -1 /var/app
ssh-privatekey
# cat /var/app/ssh-privatekey
-----BEGIN RSA PRIVATE KEY-----
Proc-Type: 4,ENCRYPTED
DEK-Info: AES-128-CBC,8734C9153079F2E8497C8075289EBBF1
...
-----END RSA PRIVATE KEY-----
```

Summary

The workload portion covered by the CKA includes the API resources Deployment, ReplicaSet, and Pod. A Deployment controls a ReplicaSet responsible for managing multiple, identical Pods, so-called replicas. The number of replicas can be scaled up or down using the Deployment manually or automatically with the help of a Horizontal Pod Autoscaler. Any changes made to the replica template defined by the Deployment will be rolled out to the replicas. As an end user, you can inspect the rollout history, the current rollout status, and its progress.

Application runtime behavior can be controlled either by injecting configuration data as environment variables or by mounting a volume to a path. In Kubernetes, this configuration data is represented by the API resources ConfigMap and Secret in the form of key-value pairs. A ConfigMap is meant for plain-text data, and a Secret encodes the values in Base64 to obfuscate the values. Secrets are usually a better fit for sensitive information like credentials and SSH private keys.

Exam Essentials

Know how to scale a Deployment and roll out updates

Deployments have superior management capabilities for a set of Pods. Using them should be preferred over creating, updating, and deleting individual Pods. You need to be familiar with all aspects of a Deployment, which includes manually scaling the number of replicas or autoscaling them with the help of a Horizontal Pod Autoscaler. The rollout history keeps track of the revisions made to a Pod template. You can roll out new revisions or roll back to a previous revision. Practice those techniques and the effect it has on the replicas.

Practice the creation and usage of ConfigMaps and Secrets

Configuration data can be injected into a Pod using a ConfigMap or a Secret. Practice the creation of those objects using the imperative and declarative approach by providing different data sources (e.g., literal values, files, and directories). Secrets offer specialized types. Try the different ways those can be set up. You need to be proficient with the different ways of injecting the data defined by ConfigMaps and Secrets into a container.

Sample Exercises

Solutions to these exercises are available in the Appendix.

1. Create a Deployment named nginx that uses the image nginx:1.17.0. Set two replicas to begin with.

2. Scale the Deployment to seven replicas using the scale command. Ensure that the correct number of Pods exist.

3. Create a Horizontal Pod Autoscaler named nginx-hpa for the Deployment with an average utilization of CPU to 65% and an average utilization of memory to 1Gi. Set the minimum number of replicas to 3 and the maximum number of replicas to 20.

4. Update the Pod template of the Deployment to use the image nginx:1.21.1. Make sure that the changes are recorded. Inspect the revision history. How many revisions should be rendered? Roll back to the first revision.

5. Create a new Secret named basic-auth of type kubernetes.io/basic-auth. Assign the key-value pairs username=super and password=my-s8cr3t. Mount the Secret as a volume with the path /etc/secret and read-only permissions to the Pods controlled by the Deployment.

## CHAPTER 4

Scheduling and Tooling

The scheduling portion of the CKA focuses on the effects of defining resource boundaries when evaluated by the Kubernetes scheduler. The default runtime behavior of the scheduler can also be modified by defining node affinity rules, as well as taints and tolerations. Of those concepts, you are expected only to understand the nuances of resource boundaries and their effect on the scheduler in different scenarios. Finally, this domain of the curriculum mentions high-level knowledge of manifest management and templating tools.

At a high level, this chapter covers the following concepts:

- Resource boundaries for Pods
- Imperative and declarative manifest management
- Common templating tools like Kustomize, yq, and Helm

Understanding How Resource Limits Affect Pod Scheduling

A Kubernetes cluster can consist of multiple nodes. Depending on a variety of rules (e.g., node selectors (*https://oreil.ly/m5eep*), node affinity (*https://oreil.ly/9Gf7E*), taints and tolerations (*https://oreil.ly/2SkeO*)), the Kubernetes scheduler decides which node to pick for running the workload. The CKA exam doesn't ask you to understand the scheduling concepts mentioned previously, but it would be helpful to have a rough idea how they work on a high level.

One metric that comes into play for workload scheduling is the resource *request* defined by the containers in a Pod. Commonly used resources that can be specified are CPU and memory. The scheduler ensures that the node's resource capacity can fulfill the resource requirements of the Pod. More specifically, the scheduler determines the sum of resource requests per type across all containers defined in the Pod and compares them with the node's available resources. Figure 4-1 illustrates the scheduling process based on the resource requests.

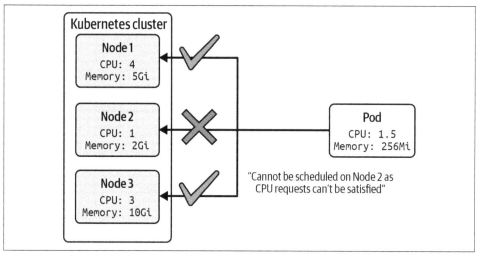

Figure 4-1. Pod scheduling based on resource requests

Defining Container Resource Requests

Each container in a Pod can define its own resource requests. Table 4-1 describes the available options including an example value.

Table 4-1. Options for resource requests

YAML Attribute	Description	Example Value
`spec.containers[].resources.requests.cpu`	CPU resource type	500m (five hundred millicpu)
`spec.containers[].resources.requests.memory`	Memory resource type	64Mi (2^{26} bytes)
`spec.containers[].resources.requests.hugepages-<size>`	Huge page resource type	huge pages-2Mi: 60Mi
`spec.containers[].resources.requests.ephemeral-storage`	Ephemeral storage resource type	4Gi

Kubernetes uses resource units for resource types that deviate from standard resource units like megabytes and gigabytes. Explaining all intricacies of those units goes beyond the scope this book, but you can read up on the details in the documentation (*https://oreil.ly/bweuT*).

To make the use of those resource requests transparent, we'll take a look at an example definition. The Pod YAML manifest shown in Example 4-1 defines two containers, each with their own resource requests. Any node that is allowed to run the Pod needs to be able to support a minimum memory capacity of 320Mi and 1250m CPU, the sum of resources across both containers.

Example 4-1. Setting container resource requests

```
apiVersion: v1
kind: Pod
metadata:
  name: rate-limiter
spec:
  containers:
  - name: business-app
    image: bmuschko/nodejs-business-app:1.0.0
    ports:
    - containerPort: 8080
    resources:
      requests:
        memory: "256Mi"
        cpu: "1"
  - name: ambassador
    image: bmuschko/nodejs-ambassador:1.0.0
    ports:
    - containerPort: 8081
    resources:
      requests:
        memory: "64Mi"
        cpu: "250m"
```

In this scenario, we are dealing with a Minikube Kubernetes cluster consisting of three nodes, one control plane node, and two worker nodes. The following command lists all nodes:

```
$ kubectl get nodes
NAME           STATUS   ROLES                   AGE   VERSION
minikube       Ready    control-plane,master    12d   v1.21.2
minikube-m02   Ready    <none>                  42m   v1.21.2
minikube-m03   Ready    <none>                  41m   v1.21.2
```

In the next step, we'll create the Pod from the YAML manifest. The scheduler places the Pod on the node named minikube-m03:

```
$ kubectl create -f rate-limiter-pod.yaml
pod/rate-limiter created
$ kubectl get pod rate-limiter -o yaml | grep nodeName:
  nodeName: minikube-m03
```

Upon further inspection of the node, you can inspect its maximum capacity, how much of this capacity is allocatable, and the memory requests of the Pods scheduled on the node. The following command lists the information and condenses the output to the relevant bits and pieces:

```
$ kubectl describe node minikube-m03
...
Capacity:
  cpu:                 2
  ephemeral-storage:   17784752Ki
  hugepages-2Mi:       0
  memory:              2186612Ki
  pods:                110
Allocatable:
  cpu:                 2
  ephemeral-storage:   17784752Ki
  hugepages-2Mi:       0
  memory:              2186612Ki
  pods:                110
...
Non-terminated Pods:            (3 in total)
  Namespace                 Name              CPU Requests  CPU Limits  \
  Memory Requests  Memory Limits  AGE
  ---------                 ----              ------------  ----------  \
  ---------------  -------------  ---
  default                   rate-limiter      1250m (62%)   0 (0%)      \
  320Mi (14%)      0 (0%)         9m
...
```

It's certainly possible that a Pod cannot be scheduled due to insufficient resources available on the nodes. In those cases, the event log of the Pod will indicate this situation with the reasons PodExceedsFreeCPU or PodExceedsFreeMemory. For more information on how to troubleshoot and resolve this situation, see the relevant section in the documentation (*https://oreil.ly/ZzK0B*).

Defining Container Resource Limits

Another metric you can set for a container are its resource *limits*. Resource limits ensure that the container cannot consume more than the allotted resource amounts. For example, you could express that the application running in the container should be constrained to 1000m of CPU and 512Mi of memory.

Depending on the container runtime used by the cluster, exceeding any of the allowed resource limits results in a termination of the application process running in the container or results in the system preventing the allocation of resources beyond the limits altogether. For an in-depth discussion on how resource limits are treated by the container runtime Docker, see the documentation (*https://oreil.ly/szUaM*).

Table 4-2 describes the available options including an example value.

Table 4-2. Options for resource limits

YAML Attribute	Description	Example Value
`spec.containers[].resources.limits.cpu`	CPU resource type	500m (500 millicpu)
`spec.containers[].resources.limits.memory`	Memory resource type	64Mi (2^26 bytes)
`spec.containers[].resources.limits.hugepages-<size>`	Huge page resource type	`hugepages-2Mi: 60Mi`
`spec.containers[].resources.limits.ephemeral-storage`	Ephemeral storage resource type	4Gi

Example 4-2 shows the definition of limits in action. Here, the container named business-app cannot use more than 512Mi of memory and 2000m of CPU. The container named ambassador defines a limit of 128Mi of memory and 500m of CPU.

Example 4-2. Setting container resource limits

```
apiVersion: v1
kind: Pod
metadata:
  name: rate-limiter
spec:
  containers:
  - name: business-app
    image: bmuschko/nodejs-business-app:1.0.0
    ports:
    - containerPort: 8080
    resources:
      limits:
        memory: "512Mi"
        cpu: "2"
  - name: ambassador
    image: bmuschko/nodejs-ambassador:1.0.0
    ports:
    - containerPort: 8081
    resources:
      limits:
        memory: "128Mi"
        cpu: "500m"
```

Assume that the Pod was scheduled on the node minikube-m03. Describing the node's details reveals that the CPU and memory limits took effect. But there's more. Kubernetes automatically assigns the same amount of resources for the requests if you only define the limits:

```
$ kubectl describe node minikube-m03
...
```

```
Non-terminated Pods:          (3 in total)
  Namespace                    Name                         CPU Requests  CPU Limits  \
  Memory Requests  Memory Limits  AGE
  ---------                    ----                         ------------  ----------  \
  ---------------  -------------  ---
  default                      rate-limiter                 1250m (62%)   1250m (62%) \
  320Mi (14%)      320Mi (14%)    11s
  ...
```

Defining Container Resource Requests and Limits

It's recommended practice that you specify resource requests and limits for every container. Determining those resource expectations is not always easy, specifically for applications that haven't been exercised in a production environment yet. Load testing the application early on during the development cycle can help with analyzing the resource needs. Further adjustments can be made by monitoring the application's resource consumption after deploying it to the cluster. Example 4-3 combines resource requests and limits in a single YAML manifest.

Example 4-3. Setting container resource requests and limits

```
apiVersion: v1
kind: Pod
metadata:
  name: rate-limiter
spec:
  containers:
  - name: business-app
    image: bmuschko/nodejs-business-app:1.0.0
    ports:
    - containerPort: 8080
    resources:
      requests:
        memory: "256Mi"
        cpu: "1"
      limits:
        memory: "512Mi"
        cpu: "2"
  - name: ambassador
    image: bmuschko/nodejs-ambassador:1.0.0
    ports:
    - containerPort: 8081
    resources:
      requests:
        memory: "64Mi"
        cpu: "250m"
      limits:
        memory: "128Mi"
        cpu: "500m"
```

As a result, you can see the different settings for resource requests and limits:

```
$ kubectl describe node minikube-m03
...
Non-terminated Pods:          (3 in total)
  Namespace                   Name                  CPU Requests  CPU Limits   \
   Memory Requests  Memory Limits  AGE
  ---------                   ----                  ------------  ----------   \
  ---------------  -------------  ---
  default                     rate-limiter          1250m (62%)   2500m (125%) \
  320Mi (14%)      640Mi (29%)    3s
...
```

Managing Objects

Kubernetes objects can be created, modified, and deleted by using imperative kubectl commands or by running a kubectl command against a configuration file declaring the desired state of an object, a so-called manifest. The primary definition language of a manifest is YAML, though you can opt for JSON, which is the less widely adopted format among the Kubernetes community. It's recommended that development teams commit and push those configuration files to version control repositories as it will help with tracking and auditing changes over time.

Modeling an application in Kubernetes often requires a set of supporting objects, each of which can have their own manifest. For example, you may want to create a Deployment that runs the application on five Pods, a ConfigMap to inject configuration data as environment variables, and a Service for exposing network access.

This section primarily focuses on the declarative object management support with the help of manifests. For a deeper discussion on the imperative support, see the relevant portions in the documentation (*https://oreil.ly/Slw0h*). Furthermore, we'll touch on tools like Kustomize and Helm to give you an impression of their benefits, capabilities, and workflows.

Declarative Object Management Using Configuration Files

Declarative object management requires one or several configuration files in the format of YAML or JSON describing the desired state of an object. You create, update, and delete objects with this approach.

Creating objects

To create new objects, run the apply command by pointing to a file, a directory of files, or a file referenced by an HTTP(S) URL using the -f option. If one or many of the objects already exist, the command will synchronize the changes made to the configuration with the live object.

To demonstrate the functionality, we'll assume the following directories and configuration files. The following commands create objects from a single file, from all files within a directory, and from all files in a directory recursively:

```
.
├── app-stack
│   ├── mysql-pod.yaml
│   ├── mysql-service.yaml
│   ├── web-app-pod.yaml
│   └── web-app-service.yaml
├── nginx-deployment.yaml
└── web-app
    ├── config
    │   ├── db-configmap.yaml
    │   └── db-secret.yaml
    └── web-app-pod.yaml
```

Creating an object from a single file:

```
$ kubectl apply -f nginx-deployment.yaml
deployment.apps/nginx-deployment created
```

Creating objects from multiple files within a directory:

```
$ kubectl apply -f app-stack/
pod/mysql-db created
service/mysql-service created
pod/web-app created
service/web-app-service created
```

Creating objects from a recursive directory tree containing files:

```
$ kubectl apply -f web-app/ -R
configmap/db-config configured
secret/db-creds created
pod/web-app created
```

Creating objects from a file referenced by an HTTP(S) URL:

```
$ kubectl apply -f https://raw.githubusercontent.com/bmuschko/cka-study-guide/ \
    master/ch04/object-management/nginx-deployment.yaml
deployment.apps/nginx-deployment created
```

The apply command keeps track of the changes by adding or modifying the annotation with the key kubectl.kubernetes.io/last-applied-configuration. You can find an example of the annotation in the output of the get pod command here:

```
$ kubectl get pod web-app -o yaml
apiVersion: v1
kind: Pod
metadata:
  annotations:
    kubectl.kubernetes.io/last-applied-configuration: |
      {"apiVersion":"v1","kind":"Pod","metadata":{"annotations":{}, \
```

```
  "labels":{"app":"web-app"},"name":"web-app","namespace":"default"}, \
  "spec":{"containers":[{"envFrom":[{"configMapRef":{"name":"db-config"}}, \
  {"secretRef":{"name":"db-creds"}}],"image":"bmuschko/web-app:1.0.1", \
  "name":"web-app","ports":[{"containerPort":3000,"protocol":"TCP"}]}], \
  "restartPolicy":"Always"}}
...
```

Updating objects

Updating an existing object is done with the same `apply` command. All you need to do is to change the configuration file and then run the command against it. Example 4-4 modifies the existing configuration of a Deployment in the file `nginx-deployment.yaml`. We added a new label with the key `team` and changed the number of replicas from 3 to 5.

Example 4-4. Modified configuration file for a Deployment

```
apiVersion: apps/v1
kind: Deployment
metadata:
  name: nginx-deployment
  labels:
    app: nginx
    team: red
spec:
  replicas: 5
...
```

The following command applies the changed configuration file. As a result, the number of Pods controlled by the underlying ReplicaSet is 5. The Deployment's annotation `kubectl.kubernetes.io/last-applied-configuration` reflects the latest change to the configuration:

```
$ kubectl apply -f nginx-deployment.yaml
deployment.apps/nginx-deployment configured
$ kubectl get deployments,pods
NAME                                READY   UP-TO-DATE   AVAILABLE   AGE
deployment.apps/nginx-deployment    5/5     5            5           10m

NAME                                    READY   STATUS    RESTARTS   AGE
pod/nginx-deployment-66b6c48dd5-79j6t   1/1     Running   0          35s
pod/nginx-deployment-66b6c48dd5-bkkgb   1/1     Running   0          10m
pod/nginx-deployment-66b6c48dd5-d26c8   1/1     Running   0          10m
pod/nginx-deployment-66b6c48dd5-fcqrs   1/1     Running   0          10m
pod/nginx-deployment-66b6c48dd5-whfnn   1/1     Running   0          35s
$ kubectl get deployment nginx-deployment -o yaml
apiVersion: apps/v1
kind: Deployment
metadata:
  annotations:
```

```
kubectl.kubernetes.io/last-applied-configuration: |
  {"apiVersion":"apps/v1","kind":"Deployment","metadata":{"annotations":{}, \
  "labels":{"app":"nginx","team":"red"},"name":"nginx-deployment", \
  "namespace":"default"},"spec":{"replicas":5,"selector":{"matchLabels": \
  {"app":"nginx"}},"template":{"metadata":{"labels":{"app":"nginx"}}, \
  "spec":{"containers":[{"image":"nginx:1.14.2","name":"nginx", \
  "ports":[{"containerPort":80}]}]}}}}
...
```

Deleting objects

While there is a way to delete objects using the `apply` command by providing the options `--prune -l <labels>`, it is recommended to delete an object using the `delete` command and point it to the configuration file. The following command deletes a Deployment and the objects it controls (ReplicaSet and Pods):

```
$ kubectl delete -f nginx-deployment.yaml
deployment.apps "nginx-deployment" deleted
$ kubectl get deployments,replicasets,pods
No resources found in default namespace.
```

Declarative Object Management Using Kustomize

Kustomize is a tool introduced with Kubernetes 1.14 that aims to make manifest management more convenient. It supports three different use cases:

- Generating manifests from other sources. For example, creating a ConfigMap and populating its key-value pairs from a properties file.

- Adding common configuration across multiple manifests. For example, adding a namespace and a set of labels for a Deployment and a Service.

- Composing and customizing a collection of manifests. For example, setting resource boundaries for multiple Deployments.

The central file needed for Kustomize to work is the *kustomization file*. The standardized name for the file is `kustomization.yaml` and cannot be changed. A kustomization file defines the processing rules Kustomize works upon.

Kustomize is fully integrated with `kubectl` and can be executed in two modes: rendering the processing output on the console or creating the objects. Both modes can operate on a directory, tarball, Git archive, or URL as long as they contain the kustomization file and referenced resource files:

Rendering the produced output
   The first mode uses the `kustomize` subcommand to render the produced result on the console but does not create the objects. This command works similar to the dry-run option you might know from the `run` command:

```
$ kubectl kustomize <target>
```

Creating the objects

The second mode uses the `apply` command in conjunction with the `-k` command-line option to apply the resources processed by Kustomize, as explained in the previous section:

```
$ kubectl apply -k <target>
```

The following sections demonstrate each of the use cases by a single example. For a full coverage on all possible scenarios, refer to the documentation (*https://oreil.ly/JUHXj*) or the Kustomize GitHub repository (*https://oreil.ly/4MirA*).

Composing Manifests

One of the core functionalities of Kustomize is to create a composed manifest from other manifests. Combining multiple manifests into a single one may not seem that useful by itself, but many of the other features described later will build upon this capability. Say you wanted to compose a manifest from a Deployment and a Service resource file. All you need to do is to place the resource files into the same folder as the kustomization file:

```
.
├── kustomization.yaml
├── web-app-deployment.yaml
└── web-app-service.yaml
```

The kustomization file lists the resources in the `resources` section, as shown in Example 4-5.

Example 4-5. A kustomization file combining two manifests

```
resources:
- web-app-deployment.yaml
- web-app-service.yaml
```

As a result, the `kustomize` subcommand renders the combined manifest containing all of the resources separated by three hyphens (`---`) to denote the different object definitions:

```
$ kubectl kustomize ./
apiVersion: v1
kind: Service
metadata:
  labels:
    app: web-app-service
  name: web-app-service
spec:
  ports:
  - name: web-app-port
```

```
      port: 3000
      protocol: TCP
      targetPort: 3000
  selector:
    app: web-app
  type: NodePort
---
apiVersion: apps/v1
kind: Deployment
metadata:
  labels:
    app: web-app-deployment
  name: web-app-deployment
spec:
  replicas: 3
  selector:
    matchLabels:
      app: web-app
  template:
    metadata:
      labels:
        app: web-app
    spec:
      containers:
      - env:
        - name: DB_HOST
          value: mysql-service
        - name: DB_USER
          value: root
        - name: DB_PASSWORD
          value: password
        image: bmuschko/web-app:1.0.1
        name: web-app
        ports:
        - containerPort: 3000
```

Generating manifests from other sources

Earlier in this chapter, we learned that ConfigMaps and Secrets can be created by pointing them to a file containing the actual configuration data for it. Kustomize can help with the process by mapping the relationship between the YAML manifest of those configuration objects and their data. Furthermore, we'll want to inject the created ConfigMap and Secret in a Pod as environment variables. In this section, you will learn how to achieve this with the help of Kustomize.

The following file and directory structure contains the manifest file for the Pod and the configuration data files we need for the ConfigMap and Secret. The mandatory kustomization file lives on the root level of the directory tree:

```
.
├── config
│   ├── db-config.properties
│   └── db-secret.properties
├── kustomization.yaml
└── web-app-pod.yaml
```

In kustomization.yaml, you can define that the ConfigMap and Secret object should be generated with the given name. The name of the ConfigMap is supposed to be db-config, and the name of the Secret is going to be db-creds. Both of the generator attributes, configMapGenerator and secretGenerator, reference an input file used to feed in the configuration data. Any additional resources can be spelled out with the resources attribute. Example 4-6 shows the contents of the kustomization file.

Example 4-6. A kustomization file using a ConfigMap and Secret generator

```
configMapGenerator:
- name: db-config
  files:
  - config/db-config.properties
secretGenerator:
- name: db-creds
  files:
  - config/db-secret.properties
resources:
- web-app-pod.yaml
```

Kustomize generates ConfigMaps and Secrets by appending a suffix to the name. You can see this behavior when creating the objects using the apply command. The ConfigMap and Secret can be referenced by name in the Pod manifest:

```
$ kubectl apply -k ./
configmap/db-config-t4c79h4mtt unchanged
secret/db-creds-4t9dmgtf9h unchanged
pod/web-app created
```

This naming strategy can be configured with the attribute generatorOptions in the kustomization file. See the documentation (*https://oreil.ly/M7tlD*) for more information.

Let's also try the `kustomize` subcommand. Instead of creating the objects, the command renders the processed output on the console:

```
$ kubectl kustomize ./
apiVersion: v1
data:
  db-config.properties: |-
    DB_HOST: mysql-service
    DB_USER: root
kind: ConfigMap
metadata:
  name: db-config-t4c79h4mtt
---
apiVersion: v1
data:
  db-secret.properties: REJfUEFTU1dPUkQ6IGNHRnpjM2R2Y21RPQ==
kind: Secret
metadata:
  name: db-creds-4t9dmgtf9h
type: Opaque
---
apiVersion: v1
kind: Pod
metadata:
  labels:
    app: web-app
  name: web-app
spec:
  containers:
  - envFrom:
    - configMapRef:
        name: db-config-t4c79h4mtt
    - secretRef:
        name: db-creds-4t9dmgtf9h
    image: bmuschko/web-app:1.0.1
    name: web-app
    ports:
    - containerPort: 3000
      protocol: TCP
  restartPolicy: Always
```

Adding common configuration across multiple manifests

Application developers usually work on an application stack set comprised of multiple manifests. For example, an application stack could consist of a frontend microservice, a backend microservice, and a database. It's common practice to use the same, cross-cutting configuration for each of the manifests. Kustomize offers a range of supported fields (e.g., namespace, labels, or annotations). Refer to the documentation (*https://oreil.ly/OyNbh*) to learn about all supported fields.

For the next example, we'll assume that a Deployment and a Service live in the same namespace and use a common set of labels. The namespace is called `persistence` and the label is the key-value pair `team: helix`. Example 4-7 illustrates how to set those common fields in the kustomization file.

Example 4-7. A kustomization file using a common field

```
namespace: persistence
commonLabels:
  team: helix
resources:
- web-app-deployment.yaml
- web-app-service.yaml
```

To create the referenced objects in the kustomization file, run the `apply` command. Make sure to create the `persistence` namespace beforehand:

```
$ kubectl create namespace persistence
namespace/persistence created
$ kubectl apply -k ./
service/web-app-service created
deployment.apps/web-app-deployment created
```

The YAML representation of the processed files looks as follows:

```
$ kubectl kustomize ./
apiVersion: v1
kind: Service
metadata:
  labels:
    app: web-app-service
    team: helix
  name: web-app-service
  namespace: persistence
spec:
  ports:
  - name: web-app-port
    port: 3000
    protocol: TCP
    targetPort: 3000
  selector:
    app: web-app
    team: helix
  type: NodePort
---
apiVersion: apps/v1
kind: Deployment
metadata:
  labels:
    app: web-app-deployment
    team: helix
```

```
    name: web-app-deployment
    namespace: persistence
spec:
  replicas: 3
  selector:
    matchLabels:
      app: web-app
      team: helix
  template:
    metadata:
      labels:
        app: web-app
        team: helix
    spec:
      containers:
      - env:
        - name: DB_HOST
          value: mysql-service
        - name: DB_USER
          value: root
        - name: DB_PASSWORD
          value: password
        image: bmuschko/web-app:1.0.1
        name: web-app
        ports:
        - containerPort: 3000
```

Customizing a collection of manifests

Kustomize can merge the contents of a YAML manifest with a code snippet
from another YAML manifest. Typical use cases include adding security context
configuration to a Pod definition or setting resource boundaries for a Deployment. The kustomization file allows for specifying different patch strategies like
patchesStrategicMerge and patchesJson6902. For a deeper discussion on the differences between patch strategies, refer to the documentation.

Example 4-8 shows the contents of a kustomization file that patches a Deployment
definition in the file nginx-deployment.yaml with the contents of the file security-
context.yaml.

Example 4-8. A kustomization file defining a patch

```
resources:
- nginx-deployment.yaml
patchesStrategicMerge:
- security-context.yaml
```

The patch file shown in Example 4-9 defines a security context on the container-level for the Pod template of the Deployment. At runtime, the patch strategy tries to find the container named `nginx` and enhances the additional configuration.

Example 4-9. The patch YAML manifest

```
apiVersion: apps/v1
kind: Deployment
metadata:
  name: nginx-deployment
spec:
  template:
    spec:
      containers:
      - name: nginx
        securityContext:
          runAsUser: 1000
          runAsGroup: 3000
          fsGroup: 2000
```

The result is a patched Deployment definition, as shown in the output of the `kustomize` subcommand shown next. The patch mechanism can be applied to other files that require a uniform security context definition:

```
$ kubectl kustomize ./
apiVersion: apps/v1
kind: Deployment
metadata:
  labels:
    app: nginx
  name: nginx-deployment
spec:
  replicas: 3
  selector:
    matchLabels:
      app: nginx
  template:
    metadata:
      labels:
        app: nginx
    spec:
      containers:
      - image: nginx:1.14.2
        name: nginx
        ports:
        - containerPort: 80
        securityContext:
          fsGroup: 2000
          runAsGroup: 3000
          runAsUser: 1000
```

Common Templating Tools

As demonstrated in the previous section, Kustomize offers templating functionality. The Kubernetes ecosystem offers other solutions to the problem that we will discuss here. We will touch on the YAML processor yq and the templating engine Helm.

Using the YAML Processor yq

The tool yq is used to read, modify, and enhance the contents of a YAML file. This section will demonstrate all three use cases. For a detailed list of usage example, see the GitHub repository (*https://oreil.ly/ORZDV*). During the CKA exam, you may be asked to apply those techniques though you are not expected to understand all intricacies of the tools at hand. The version of yq used to describe the functionality below is 4.2.1.

Reading values

Reading values from an existing YAML file requires the use of a YAML path expression. A path expression allows you to deeply navigate the YAML structure and extract the value of an attribute you are searching for. Example 4-10 shows the YAML manifest of a Pod that defines two environment variables.

Example 4-10. The YAML manifest of a Pod

```
apiVersion: v1
kind: Pod
metadata:
  name: spring-boot-app
spec:
  containers:
  - image: bmuschko/spring-boot-app:1.5.3
    name: spring-boot-app
    env:
    - name: SPRING_PROFILES_ACTIVE
      value: prod
    - name: VERSION
      value: '1.5.3'
```

To read a value, use the command `eval` or the short form `e`, provide the YAML path expression, and point it to the source file. The following two commands read the Pod's name and the value of the second environment variable defined by a single container. Notice that the path expression needs to start with a mandatory dot character (`.`) to denote the root node of the YAML structure:

```
$ yq e .metadata.name pod.yaml
spring-boot-app
$ yq e .spec.containers[0].env[1].value pod.yaml
1.5.3
```

Modifying values

Modifying an existing value is as easy as using the same command and adding the `-i`
flag. The assignment of the new value to an attribute happens by assigning it to the
path expression. The following command changes the second environment variable
of the Pod YAML file to the value 1.6.0:

```
$ yq e -i .spec.containers[0].env[1].value = "1.6.0" pod.yaml
$ cat pod.yaml
...
    env:
    - name: SPRING_PROFILES_ACTIVE
      value: prod
    - name: VERSION
      value: 1.6.0
```

Merging YAML files

Similar to Kustomize, yq can merge multiple YAML files. Kustomize is definitely
more powerful and convenient to use; however, yq can come in handy for smaller
projects. Say you wanted to merge the sidecar container definition shown in Example 4-11 into the Pod YAML file.

Example 4-11. The YAML manifest of a container definition

```
spec:
  containers:
  - image: envoyproxy/envoy:v1.19.1
    name: proxy-container
    ports:
    - containerPort: 80
```

The command to achieve this is `eval-all`. We won't go into details given the multitude of configuration options for this command. For a deep dive, check the yq user
manual on the "Multiply (Merge)" operation (*https://oreil.ly/2I6ir*). The following
command appends the sidecar container to the existing container array of the Pod
manifest:

```
$ yq eval-all 'select(fileIndex == 0) *+ select(fileIndex == 1)' pod.yaml \
  sidecar.yaml
apiVersion: v1
kind: Pod
metadata:
  name: spring-boot-app
```

```
spec:
  containers:
  - image: bmuschko/spring-boot-app:1.5.3
    name: spring-boot-app
    env:
    - name: SPRING_PROFILES_ACTIVE
      value: prod
    - name: VERSION
      value: '1.5.3'
  - image: envoyproxy/envoy:v1.19.1
    name: proxy-container
    ports:
    - containerPort: 80
```

Using Helm

Helm (*https://helm.sh*) is a templating engine and package manager for a set of Kubernetes manifests. At runtime, it replaces placeholders in YAML template files with actual, end-user defined values. The artifact produced by the Helm executable is a so-called *chart file* bundling the manifests that comprise the API resources of an application. This chart file can be uploaded to a package manager to be used during the deployment process. The Helm ecosystem offers a wide range of reusable charts for common use cases on a central chart repository (*https://oreil.ly/1OLIi*) (e.g., for running Grafana or PostgreSQL).

Due to the wealth of functionality available to Helm, we'll discuss only the very basics. The CKA exam does not expect you be a Helm expert; rather, it wants to be familiar with the benefits and concepts. For more detailed information on Helm, see the user documentation (*https://helm.sh/docs*). The version of Helm used to describe the functionality here is 3.7.0.

Standard Chart Structure

A chart needs to follow a predefined directory structure. You can choose any name for the root directory. Within the directory, two files need to exist: `Chart.yaml` and `values.yaml`. The file `Chart.yaml` describes the meta information of the chart (e.g., name and version). The file `values.yaml` contains the key-value pairs used at runtime to replace the placeholders in the YAML manifests. Any template file meant to be packaged into the chart archive file needs to be put in the `templates` directory. Files located in the `template` directory do not have to follow any naming conventions.

The following directory structure shows an example chart. The `templates` directory contains a file for a Pod and a Service:

```
$ tree
.
├── Chart.yaml
├── templates
│   ├── web-app-pod-template.yaml
│   └── web-app-service-template.yaml
└── values.yaml
```

The chart file

The file `Chart.yaml` describes the chart on a high level. Mandatory attributes include the chart's API version, the name, and the version. Additionally, optional attributes can be provided. For a full list of attributes, see the relevant documentation (*https://oreil.ly/VUrm1*). Example 4-12 shows the bare minimum of a chart file.

Example 4-12. A basic Helm chart file

```
apiVersion: 1.0.0
name: web-app
version: 2.5.4
```

The values file

The file `values.yaml` defines key-value pairs to be used to replace placeholders in the YAML template files. Example 4-13 specifies four key-value pairs. Be aware that the file can be empty if you don't want to replace values at runtime.

Example 4-13. A Helm values file

```
db_host: mysql-service
db_user: root
db_password: password
service_port: 3000
```

The template files

Template files need to live in the `templates` directory. A template file is a regular YAML manifest that can (optionally) define placeholders with the help of double curly braces (`{{ }}`). To reference a value from the `values.yaml` file, use the expression `{{ .Values.<key> }}`. For example, to replace the value of the key db_host at runtime, use the expression `{{ .Values.db_host }}`. Example 4-14 defines a Pod as a template while defining three placeholders that reference values from `values.yaml`.

Example 4-14. The YAML template manifest of a Pod

```yaml
apiVersion: v1
kind: Pod
metadata:
  labels:
    app: web-app
  name: web-app
spec:
  containers:
  - image: bmuschko/web-app:1.0.1
    name: web-app
    env:
    - name: DB_HOST
      value: {{ .Values.db_host }}
    - name: DB_USER
      value: {{ .Values.db_user }}
    - name: DB_PASSWORD
      value: {{ .Values.db_password }}
    ports:
    - containerPort: 3000
      protocol: TCP
  restartPolicy: Always
```

Executing Helm commands

The Helm executable comes with a wide range of commands. Let's demonstrate some of them. The `template` command renders the chart templates locally and displays results on the console. You can see the operation in action in the following output. All placeholders have been replaced by their actual values sourced from the `values.yaml` file:

```
$ helm template .
---
# Source: Web Application/templates/web-app-service-template.yaml
...
---
# Source: Web Application/templates/web-app-pod-template.yaml
apiVersion: v1
kind: Pod
metadata:
  labels:
    app: web-app
  name: web-app
spec:
  containers:
  - image: bmuschko/web-app:1.0.1
    name: web-app
    env:
    - name: DB_HOST
      value: mysql-service
```

```
  - name: DB_USER
    value: root
  - name: DB_PASSWORD
    value: password
  ports:
  - containerPort: 3000
    protocol: TCP
  restartPolicy: Always
```

Once you are happy with the result, you'll want to bundle the template files into a chart archive file. The chart archive file is a compressed TAR file with the file ending `.tgz`. The `package` command evaluates the metadata information from `Chart.yaml` to derive the chart archive filename:

```
$ helm package .
Successfully packaged chart and saved it to: /Users/bmuschko/dev/projects/ \
cka-study-guide/ch04/templating-tools/helm/web-app-2.5.4.tgz
```

For a full list of commands and typical workflows, refer to the Helm documentation page (*https://oreil.ly/Jz6eD*).

Summary

Resource boundaries are one of the many factors that the kube-scheduler algorithm considers when making decisions on which node a Pod can be scheduled. A container can specify resource requests and limits. The scheduler chooses a node based on its available hardware capacity.

Declarative manifest management is the preferred way of creating, modifying, and deleting objects in real-world, cloud-native projects. The underlying YAML manifest is meant to be checked into version control and automatically tracks the changes made to a object including its timestamp for a corresponding commit hash. The `kubectl apply` and `delete` command can perform those operations for one or many YAML manifests.

Additional tools emerged for more convenient manifest management. Kustomize is fully integrated with the `kubectl` tool chain. It helps with the generation, composition, and customization of manifests. Tools with templating capabilities like yq and Helm can further ease various workflows for managing application stacks represented by a set of manifests.

Exam Essentials

Understand the effects of resource boundaries on scheduling

A container defined by a Pod can specify resource requests and limits. Work through scenarios where you define those boundaries individually and together for single- and multi-container Pods. Upon creation of the Pod, you should be able to see the effects on scheduling the object on a node. Furthermore, practice how to identify the available resource capacity of a node.

Manage objects using the imperative and declarative approach
YAML manifests are essential for expressing the desired state of an object. You will need to understand how to create, update, and delete objects using the kubectl apply command. The command can point to a single manifest file or a directory containing multiple manifest files.

Have a high-level understanding of common templating tools
Kustomize, yg, and Helm are established tools for managing YAML manifests. Their templating functionality supports complex scenarios like composing and merging multiple manifests. For the exam, take a practical look at the tools, their functionality, and the problems they solve.

Sample Exercises

Solutions to these exercises are available in the Appendix.

1. Write a manifest for a new Pod named ingress-controller with a single container that uses the image bitnami/nginx-ingress-controller:1.0.0. For the container, set the resource request to 256Mi for memory and 1 CPU. Set the resource limits to 1024Mi for memory and 2.5 CPU.

2. Using the manifest, schedule the Pod on a cluster with three nodes. Once created, identify the node that runs the Pod. Write the node name to the file node.txt.

3. Create the directory named manifests. Within the directory, create two files: pod.yaml and configmap.yaml. The pod.yaml file should define a Pod named nginx with the image nginx:1.21.1. The configmap.yaml file defines a ConfigMap named logs-config with the key-value pair dir=/etc/logs/traffic.log. Create both objects with a single, declarative command.

4. Modify the ConfigMap manifest by changing the value of the key dir to /etc/logs/traffic-log.txt. Apply the changes. Delete both objects with a single declarative command.

5. Use Kustomize to set a common namespace t012 for the resource file pod.yaml. The file pod.yaml defines the Pod named nginx with the image nginx:1.21.1 without a namespace. Run the Kustomize command that renders the transformed manifest on the console.

## CHAPTER 5

Services and Networking

Applications running in a Kubernetes cluster rarely work in isolation. In the constellation of a microservices architecture, a set of applications running in their corresponding Pods need to work together. Kubernetes enables intracluster Pod-to-Service communication and communication with select Services from outside of the cluster with the help of various networking concepts. This domain of the CKA focuses on Services and networking aspects. You will need to understand the concept of a Service and an Ingress, as well as the cluster configuration that enables network communication.

At a high level, this chapter covers the following concepts:

- Kubernetes networking basics
- Connectivity between Pods
- Services, service types and their endpoints
- Ingress controller and Ingress
- Using and configuring CoreDNS
- Choosing a container network interface (CNI) plugin

Kubernetes Networking Basics

Kubernetes is designed as an operating system for managing the complexities of distributed data and computing. Workloads can be scheduled on a set of nodes to distribute the load. The Kubernetes network model enables networking communication and needs to fulfill the following requirements:

1. Container-to-container communication: Containers running in a Pod often need to communicate with each other. Containers within the same Pods can send Inter Process Communication (IPC) messages, share files, and most often communicate directly through the loopback interface using the `localhost` hostname. Because each Pod is assigned a unique virtual IP address, each container in the same Pod is given that context and shares the same port space.

2. Pod-to-Pod communication: A Pod needs to be able to reach another Pod running on the same or on a different node without Network Address Translation (NAT). Kubernetes assigns a unique IP address to every Pod upon creation from the Pod CIDR range of its node. The IP address is ephemeral and therefore cannot be considered stable over time. Every restart of a Pod leases a new IP address. It's recommended to use Pod-to-Service communication over Pod-to-Pod communication.

3. Pod-to-Service communication: Services expose a single, stable DNS name for a set of Pods with the capability of load balancing the requests across the Pods. Traffic to a Service can be received from within the cluster or from the outside.

4. Node-to-node communication: Nodes registered with a cluster can talk to each other. Every node is assigned a node IP address.

The specification for the Kubernetes networking model is called Container Network Interface (CNI). Network plugins that implement the CNI specification are widely available and can be configured in a Kubernetes cluster by the administrator.

Connectivity Between Containers

Containers created by a single Pod share the same IP address and port space. Containers can communicate among each other using `localhost`. That's especially useful when creating cloud-native applications that require implementing a multi-container pattern, as shown in Figure 5-1. Refer to the book *Kubernetes Patterns* (O'Reilly) for more information on common multi-container design patterns.

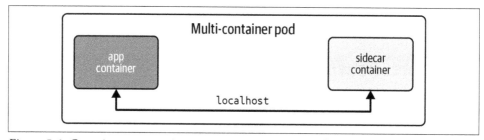

Figure 5-1. Container-to-container communication in a Pod

The YAML manifest in Example 5-1 creates a sidecar container that calls the main application container via `localhost` on port 80:

Example 5-1. A multi-container Pod

```
apiVersion: v1
kind: Pod
metadata:
  name: multi-container
spec:
  containers:
  - image: nginx
    name: app
    ports:
    - containerPort: 80
  - image: curlimages/curl:7.79.1
    name: sidecar
    args:
    - /bin/sh
    - -c
    - 'while true; do curl localhost:80; sleep 5; done;'
```

Checking the logs of the sidecar container shows that the communication to the main application container was successful:

```
$ kubectl create -f pod.yaml
pod/multi-container created
$ kubectl logs multi-container -c sidecar
...
<!DOCTYPE html>
<html>
<head>
<title>Welcome to nginx!</title>
...
```

Connectivity Between Pods

Every Pod is assigned an IP address upon creation. You can inspect a Pod's IP address by using the `-o wide` command-line option for the `get pods` command or by describing the Pod. The IP address of the Pod in the following console output is `172.17.0.4`:

```
$ kubectl run nginx --image=nginx --port=80
pod/nginx created
$ kubectl get pod nginx -o wide
NAME    READY    STATUS    RESTARTS    AGE    IP            NODE        \
NOMINATED NODE    READINESS GATES
nginx    1/1    Running    0    37s    172.17.0.4    minikube    \
<none>            <none>
$ kubectl get pod nginx -o yaml
```

```
...
status:
  podIP: 172.17.0.4
...
```

The IP address assigned to a Pod is unique across all nodes and namespaces. This is achieved by assigning a dedicated subnet to each node when registering it. When creating a new Pod on a node, the IP address is leased from the assigned subnet. This is handled by the networking lifecycle manager kube-proxy along with the DNS service and the CNI. The following command queries the assigned subnet via the attribute spec.podCIDR from the node named minikube:

```
$ kubectl get nodes
NAME       STATUS   ROLES                  AGE   VERSION
minikube   Ready    control-plane,master   42d   v1.21.2
$ kubectl get nodes minikube -o json | jq .spec.podCIDR
"172.17.0.0/24"
```

Pods on a node can communicate with all other Pods running on any other node of the cluster. Figure 5-2 illustrates the use case.

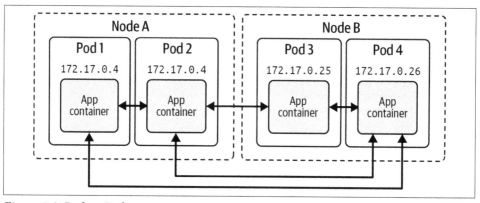

Figure 5-2. Pod-to-Pod communication

You can easily verify the behavior by creating a temporary Pod that calls the IP address of another Pod using the command-line tool curl or wget:

```
$ kubectl run busybox --image=busybox --rm -it --restart=Never \
  -- wget 172.17.0.4:80
Connecting to 172.17.0.4:80 (172.17.0.4:80)
saving to 'index.html'
index.html           100% |*****************************|   615  0:00:00 ETA
'index.html' saved
pod "busybox" deleted
```

It's important to understand that the IP address is not considered stable over time. A Pod restart leases a new IP address. Building a microservices architecture, where each of the applications runs in its own Pod with the need to communicate between each other with a stable network interface, requires a different concept, the Service.

Understanding Services

In a nutshell, Services provide discoverable names and load balancing to a set of Pods. The Services and Pods remain agnostic from IP addresses with the help of the Kubernetes DNS control-plane component. Similar to a Deployment, the Service determines the Pods it works on with the help of label selection.

Figure 5-3 illustrates the functionality. Pod 1 receives traffic as its assigned labels match with the label selection defined in the Service. Pod 2 does not receive traffic as it defines nonmatching labels. Note that it is possible to create a Service without a label selector for less-common scenarios. Refer to the relevant Kubernetes documentation (*https://oreil.ly/lCzAa*) for more information.

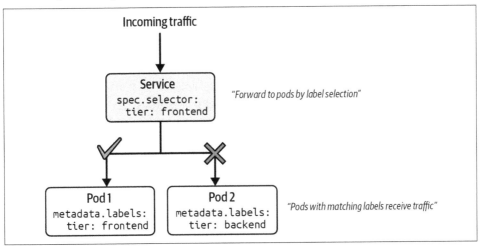

Figure 5-3. Service traffic routing based on label selection

Services are a complementary concept to Deployments. Services route network traffic to a set of Pods, and Deployments manage a set of Pods, the replicas. While you can use both concepts in isolation, it is recommended to use Deployments and Services together. The primary reason is the ability to scale the number of replicas and at the same time expose an endpoint to control network traffic.

Service Types

Every Service needs to define a type. Table 5-1 lists the Service types relevant to the CKA exam.

Table 5-1. Service types

Type	Description
ClusterIP	Exposes the Service on a cluster-internal IP. Only reachable from within the cluster.
NodePort	Exposes the Service on each node's IP address at a static port. Accessible from outside of the cluster.
LoadBalancer	Exposes the Service externally using a cloud provider's load balancer.

Other Service types can be defined; however, we'll not address them in this book as they are out of scope for the exam. For more information, refer to the Kubernetes documentation (*https://oreil.ly/3jzod*).

Creating Services

You can create Services in a variety of ways, some of which are more conducive to the CKA exam as they provide a fast turnaround. Let's discuss the imperative approach first.

A Service needs to select a Pod by a matching label. The Pod created by the following `run` command is called `echoserver`, which exposes the application on the container port 8080. Internally, it automatically assigns the label key-value pair `run:echoserver` to the object:

```
$ kubectl run echoserver --image=k8s.gcr.io/echoserver:1.10 --restart=Never \
  --port=8080
pod/echoserver created
```

The `create service` command creates the corresponding Service object. You need to provide the Service type as a mandatory argument. Here we are using the type `clusterip`. The command-line option `--tcp` specifies the port mapping, port 80 exposed by the Service for incoming network traffic and port 8080, which targets the container port exposed by the Pod:

```
$ kubectl create service clusterip echoserver --tcp=80:8080
service/echoserver created
```

An even faster workflow of creating a Pod and Service together can be achieved with the option `--expose` for the `run` command. The following command creates both objects in one swoop while creating the proper label selection. This command-line option is a good choice during the CKA to save time if you were asked to create a Pod and a Service:

```
$ kubectl run echoserver --image=k8s.gcr.io/echoserver:1.10 --restart=Never \
  --port=8080 --expose
service/echoserver created
pod/echoserver created
```

It's actually more common to use a Deployment and Service that work together. The following set of commands creates a Deployment with five replicas and then uses the expose deployment command to create the Service. The port mapping can be provided with the options --port and --target-port:

```
$ kubectl create deployment echoserver --image=k8s.gcr.io/echoserver:1.10 \
  --replicas=5
deployment.apps/echoserver created
$ kubectl expose deployment echoserver --port=80 --target-port=8080
service/echoserver exposed
```

Example 5-2 shows the representation of a Service in the form of a YAML manifest. The Service declares the key-value app: echoserver for label selection and defines the port mapping 80 to 8080.

Example 5-2. A Service defined by a YAML manifest

```
apiVersion: v1
kind: Service
metadata:
  name: echoserver
spec:
  type: ClusterIP
  selector:
    app: echoserver
  ports:
  - port: 80
    targetPort: 8080
```

Listing Services

Listing all Services presents a table view that includes the Service type, the cluster IP address, and the incoming port. Here, you can see the output for the echoserver Pod we created earlier:

```
$ kubectl get services
NAME         TYPE        CLUSTER-IP      EXTERNAL-IP   PORT(S)   AGE
echoserver   ClusterIP   10.109.241.68   <none>        80/TCP    6s
```

Rendering Service Details

You may want to drill into the details of a Service for troubleshooting purposes. That might be the case if the incoming traffic to a Service isn't routed properly to the set of Pods you expect to handle the workload.

The describe command renders valuable information about the configuration of a Service. The configuration relevant to troubleshooting a Service is the value of the fields Selector, IP, Port, TargetPort, and Endpoints.

Take a look at the output of the following describe command. It's the details for a Service created for five Pods controlled by a Deployment. The Endpoints attribute lists a range of endpoints, one for each of the Pods:

```
$ kubectl describe service echoserver
Name:              echoserver
Namespace:         default
Labels:            app=echoserver
Annotations:       <none>
Selector:          app=echoserver
Type:              ClusterIP
IP Family Policy:  SingleStack
IP Families:       IPv4
IP:                10.109.241.68
IPs:               10.109.241.68
Port:              <unset>  80/TCP
TargetPort:        8080/TCP
Endpoints:         172.17.0.4:8080,172.17.0.5:8080,172.17.0.7:8080 + 2 more...
Session Affinity:  None
Events:            <none>
```

Kubernetes represents endpoints by a dedicated resource that you can query for. The endpoint object is created at the same time you create the Service object. The following command lists the endpoint for the Service named echoserver:

```
$ kubectl get endpoints echoserver
NAME         ENDPOINTS                                                       AGE
echoserver   172.17.0.4:8080,172.17.0.5:8080,172.17.0.7:8080 + 2 more...   8m5s
```

The details of the endpoint give away the full list of IP address and port combinations:

```
$ kubectl describe endpoint echoserver
Name:         echoserver
Namespace:    default
Labels:       app=echoserver
Annotations:  endpoints.kubernetes.io/last-change-trigger-time: \
              2021-11-15T19:09:04Z
Subsets:
  Addresses:          172.17.0.4,172.17.0.5,172.17.0.7,172.17.0.8,172.17.0.9
  NotReadyAddresses:  <none>
```

```
Ports:
   Name     Port  Protocol
   ----     ----  --------
   <unset>  8080  TCP

Events:  <none>
```

Port Mapping

A Service selects the set of Pods to forward traffic to by the assigned labels. Successful routing of network traffic also depends on the proper port mapping. In the previous sections, we created different Services and assigned ports to them. Here, we'll want to revisit the port mapping by making its moving parts more transparent.

Figure 5-4 shows a Service that accepts incoming traffic on port 80. That's the port defined by the attribute `spec.ports[].port` in the manifest. Any incoming traffic is then routed toward the target port, represented by `spec.ports[].targetPort`. The target port is the same port as defined by the container running inside the label-selected Pod. In this case, that's port 8080.

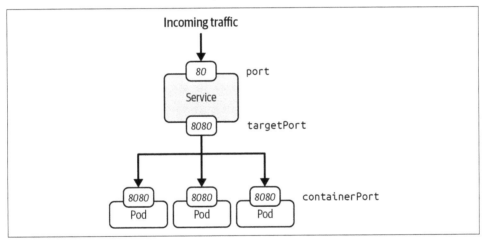

Figure 5-4. Service port mapping

Accessing a Service with Type ClusterIP

`ClusterIP` is the default type of Service. It exposes the Service on a cluster-internal IP address. That means the Service can be accessed only from a Pod running inside of the cluster but not from outside of the cluster (e.g., if you were to make call to the Service from your local machine). Figure 5-5 illustrates the accessibility of a Service with type `ClusterIP`.

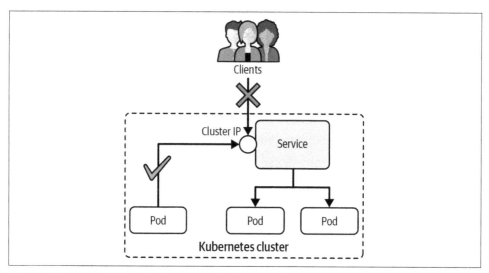

Figure 5-5. Accessibility of a Service with the type `ClusterIP`

We will create a Pod and a corresponding Service to demonstrate the runtime behavior of `ClusterIP`. The Pod named `echoserver` exposes the container port 8080 and specifies the label `app: echoserver`. The Service defines port 5005 for incoming traffic, which is forwarded to port 8080 for the Pod selected. The label selection matches the Pod we set up:

```
$ kubectl run echoserver --image=k8s.gcr.io/echoserver:1.10 --restart=Never \
  --port=8080 -l app=echoserver
pod/echoserver created
$ kubectl create service clusterip echoserver --tcp=5005:8080
service/echoserver created
```

The cluster IP that makes the Service available is `10.96.254.0`. Listing the Service also renders the port for incoming traffic to the Service:

```
$ kubectl get pod,service
NAME             READY   STATUS    RESTARTS   AGE
pod/echoserver   1/1     Running   0          23s

NAME                 TYPE        CLUSTER-IP     EXTERNAL-IP   PORT(S)    AGE
service/echoserver   ClusterIP   10.96.254.0    <none>        5005/TCP   8s
```

You cannot access the Service using the cluster IP and the port from your local machine, illustrated by the following `wget` command:

```
$ wget 10.96.254.0:5005 --timeout=5 --tries=1
--2021-11-15 15:45:36--  http://10.96.254.0:5005/
Connecting to 10.96.254.0:5005... ]failed: Operation timed out.
Giving up.
```

Accessing the Service from a temporary Pod from within the cluster properly routes
the request to the Pod matching the label selection:

```
$ kubectl run tmp --image=busybox --restart=Never -it --rm \
  -- wget 10.96.254.0:5005
Connecting to 10.96.254.0:5005 (10.96.254.0:5005)
saving to 'index.html'
index.html           100% |*******************************|   408  0:00:00 ETA
'index.html' saved
pod "tmp" deleted
```

Accessing a Service with Type NodePort

Declaring a Service with type NodePort exposes access through the node's IP
address and can be resolved from outside of the Kubernetes cluster. The node's IP
address can be reached in combination with a port number in the range of 30000 and
32767, assigned automatically upon the creation of the Service. This port is opened
on every node in the cluster, and its value is global and unique at the cluster-scope
level. To avoid port conflicts, it's best to not define the exact node port and let
Kubernetes find an available port. Keep in mind NodePort (capital N) is the Service
type, whereas nodePort (lowercase n) is the key for the value. Figure 5-6 illustrates
the routing of traffic to Pods via a NodePort-typed Service.

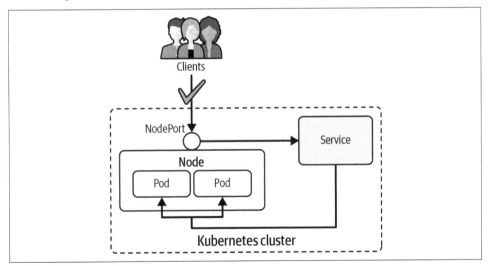

Figure 5-6. Accessibility of a Service with the type NodePort

The next two commands create a Pod and a Service of type NodePort. The only difference here is to provide nodeport instead of clusterip as a command-line option:

```
$ kubectl run echoserver --image=k8s.gcr.io/echoserver:1.10 --restart=Never \
  --port=8080 -l app=echoserver
pod/echoserver created
$ kubectl create service nodeport echoserver --tcp=5005:8080
service/echoserver created
```

Once they're created, you can list the Pods and Services. You will find that the port representation contains the statically assigned port that makes the Service accessible. In our case, that's port 30158:

```
$ kubectl get pod,service
NAME            READY   STATUS    RESTARTS   AGE
pod/echoserver  1/1     Running   0          17s

NAME                 TYPE       CLUSTER-IP      EXTERNAL-IP   PORT(S)        \
AGE
service/echoserver   NodePort   10.101.184.152  <none>        5005:30158/TCP \
5s
```

From within the cluster, you can still access the Service using the cluster IP address and port number. This Services exposes exactly the same behavior as if it were of type ClusterIP:

```
$ kubectl run tmp --image=busybox --restart=Never -it --rm \
  -- wget 10.101.184.152:5005
Connecting to 10.101.184.152:5005 (10.101.184.152:5005)
saving to 'index.html'
index.html           100% |********************************|   414  0:00:00 ETA
'index.html' saved
pod "tmp" deleted
```

From outside of the cluster, you need to use the IP address of the node running the Pod and the statically assigned port. One way to determine the node's IP address is via kubectl cluster-info or by querying the Pod.

Determining the Service URL in Minikube

Minikube offers a shortcut for determining the Service endpoint via the command minikube service --url <service-name>. For more information, see the Minikube documentation (*https://oreil.ly/HGYRp*).

The node IP address here is 192.168.64.15. It can be used to call the Service from outside of the cluster:

```
$ kubectl get nodes -o \
  jsonpath='{ $.items[*].status.addresses[?(@.type=="InternalIP")].address }'
192.168.64.15
$ wget 192.168.64.15:30158
--2021-11-16 14:10:16--  http://192.168.64.15:30158/
Connecting to 192.168.64.15:30158... connected.
HTTP request sent, awaiting response... 200 OK
Length: unspecified [text/plain]
Saving to: 'index.html'
...
```

Accessing a Service with Type LoadBalancer

Kubernetes cloud providers offer support for configuration from a preexisting external load balancer to a Service with the help of the type LoadBalancer. This Service type exposes a single IP address that distributes incoming requests to the cluster nodes. The implementation of the load balancing strategy (e.g., round robin) is up to the cloud provider. Figure 5-7 shows an architectural overview.

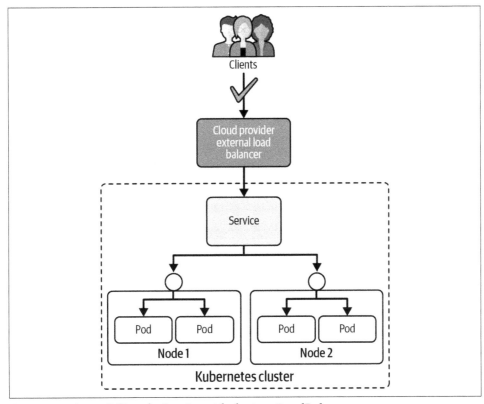

Figure 5-7. Accessibility of a Service with the type LoadBalancer

Setting up a network route in Minikube

Minikube is not a cloud provider implementation of Kubernetes; however, you can configure a network route to the Service to try out load balancer functionality. All you need to do is to run the command minikube tunnel in a separate shell. For more information, see the Minikube documentation (*https://oreil.ly/O37FF*).

To create a Service as a load balancer, set the type to LoadBalancer in the manifest or by using the create service loadbalancer command:

```
$ kubectl run echoserver --image=k8s.gcr.io/echoserver:1.10 --restart=Never \
  --port=8080 -l app=echoserver
pod/echoserver created
 $ kubectl create service loadbalancer echoserver --tcp=5005:8080
service/echoserver created
```

You will find that a Service of type LoadBalancer exposes an external IP address. List the Service to render the external IP address, which is 10.109.76.157 in the following output:

```
$ kubectl get pod,service
NAME             READY    STATUS    RESTARTS    AGE
pod/echoserver   1/1      Running   0           9s

NAME                   TYPE           CLUSTER-IP      EXTERNAL-IP   \
PORT(S)          AGE
service/echoserver     LoadBalancer   10.109.76.157   10.109.76.157 \
5005:30642/TCP   5s
```

To call the Service from outside of the cluster, use the external IP address and its incoming port:

```
$ wget 10.109.76.157:5005
--2021-11-17 11:30:44--  http://10.109.76.157:5005/
Connecting to 10.109.76.157:5005... connected.
HTTP request sent, awaiting response... 200 OK
Length: unspecified [text/plain]
Saving to: 'index.html'
...
```

Understanding Ingress

Standard Kubernetes Ingress solutions provide load balancing only at layer 7 (HTTP or HTTPS traffic) and route transactions from outside of the cluster to Services within the cluster, as illustrated in Figure 5-8. It's not a specific Service type, nor should it be confused with the Service type LoadBalancer.

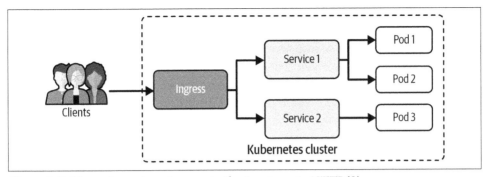

Figure 5-8. Managing external access to the Services via HTTP(S)

An Ingress cannot work without an Ingress controller. The Ingress controller evaluates the collection of rules defined by an Ingress that determine traffic routing. One example of a production-grade Ingress controller is the F5 NGINX Ingress Controller (*https://oreil.ly/owWZN*) or AKS Application Gateway Ingress Controller (*https://oreil.ly/8hupA*). You can find other options listed in the Kubernetes documentation (*https://oreil.ly/wGHWl*).

Ingress functionality has to be enabled explicitly if you are using Minikube. The Ingress controller runs as a Pod in the namespace `ingress-nginx`:

```
$ minikube addons enable ingress
$ kubectl get pods -n ingress-nginx
NAME                                      READY  STATUS    RESTARTS  AGE
ingress-nginx-controller-59b45fb494-xpfzn  0/1    Running   0         14s
```

Ingress Rules

Rules defined by an Ingress object follow the three criteria listed in Table 5-2.

Table 5-2. Ingress rules

Type	Example	Description
An optional host	`mycom pany.abc.com`	If a host is provided, then the rules apply to that host. If no host is defined, then all inbound HTTP(S) traffic is handled.
A list of paths	`/corellian/api`	Incoming traffic must match the host and path to correctly forward the traffic to a Service.
The backend	`corellian:8080`	A combination of Service name and port.

Creating Ingresses

You can create an Ingress with the imperative `create ingress` command. The main command-line option you will need to provide is `--rule`, which defines the rules in a comma-separated fashion. The notation for each key-value pair is `<host>/<path>=<service>:<port>`. If you look at the output of the `create ingress --help` command, more fine-grained rules can be specified:

```
$ kubectl create ingress corellian \
    --rule="star-alliance.com/corellian/api=corellian:8080"
ingress.networking.k8s.io/corellian created
```

 Port 80 for HTTP traffic is implied as we didn't specify a reference to a TLS Secret object. If you would have specified `tls=mysecret` in the rule definition, then the port 443 would be listed here as well. For more information on enabling HTTPS traffic, see the Kubernetes documentation (*https://oreil.ly/d2sbY*).

The same Ingress defined as a YAML manifest is shown in Example 5-3.

Example 5-3. An Ingress defined by a YAML manifest

```
apiVersion: networking.k8s.io/v1
kind: Ingress
metadata:
  name: corellian
spec:
  rules:
  - host: star-alliance.com
    http:
      paths:
      - backend:
          service:
            name: corellian
            port:
              number: 8080
        path: /corellian/api
        pathType: Exact
```

Defining Path Types

The previous YAML manifest demonstrates one of the options for specifying a path type via the attribute `spec.rules[].host[].http.paths[].pathType`. The path type defines how an incoming request is evaluated against the declared path. Table 5-3 should give you an indication on the evaluation for incoming requests and their paths. See the Kubernetes documentation (*https://oreil.ly/4plCE*) for a more comprehensive list.

Table 5-3. Ingress path types

Path Type	Rule	Incoming Request
Exact	/corellian/api	Matches /corellian/api but does not match /corellian/test or /corellian/api/
Prefix	/corellian/api	Matches /corellian/api and /corellian/api/ but does not match /corellian/test

Listing Ingresses

Listing Ingresses can be achieved with the get ingress command. You will see some of the information you specified when creating the Ingress (e.g., the hosts):

```
$ kubectl get ingress
NAME        CLASS    HOSTS              ADDRESS         PORTS   AGE
corellian   <none>   star-alliance.com  192.168.64.15   80      10m
```

Rendering Ingress Details

The details of an Ingress can be rendered using the describe ingress command. Each of the rules is listed in a table. For troubleshooting purposes, look out for additional messages. In the following output, you can see that the Service named corellian we mapped here does not exist. Furthermore, the event log shows syncing activity of the rules by the Ingress controller:

```
$ kubectl describe ingress corellian
Name:            corellian
Namespace:       default
Address:
Default backend: default-http-backend:80 (<error: endpoints \
                 "default-http-backend" not found>)
Rules:
  Host              Path  Backends
  ----              ----  --------
  star-alliance.com
                    /corellian/api   corellian:8080 (<error: \
                    endpoints "corellian" not found>)
Annotations:        <none>
Events:
  Type    Reason  Age   From                      Message
  ----    ------  ----  ----                      -------
  Normal  Sync    13s   nginx-ingress-controller  Scheduled for sync
```

With the Service and Pod serving up a request, here are the Ingress details:

```
$ kubectl run corellian --image=k8s.gcr.io/echoserver:1.10 --restart=Never \
  --port=8080 -l app=corellian
pod/corellian created
$ kubectl create service clusterip corellian --tcp=8080:8080
service/corellian created
$ kubectl describe ingress corellian
Name:           corellian
Namespace:      default
Address:        192.168.64.15
Default backend: default-http-backend:80 (<error: \
                endpoints "default-http-backend" not found>)
Rules:
  Host                  Path  Backends
  ----                  ----  --------
  star-alliance.com
                        /corellian/api    corellian:8080 (172.17.0.5:8080)
Annotations:            <none>
Events:                 <none>
```

Accessing an Ingress

The combination of backend and path routes incoming HTTP(S) traffic through the Ingress, which in turn propagates the call to the configured Service. To test the behavior on a local Kubernetes cluster on your machine, you need to first find out the IP address of the load balancer used by the Ingress. Next, you'll need to add the IP address to hostname mapping to your /etc/hosts file:

```
$ kubectl get ingress corellian \
  --output=jsonpath="{.status.loadBalancer.ingress[0][ip]}"
192.168.64.15
$ sudo vim /etc/hosts
...
192.168.64.15   star-alliance.com
```

You can now send HTTP requests to the backend. The first call matches the Exact path rule. The second call doesn't go through as the path rule does not match:

```
$ wget star-alliance.com/corellian/api --timeout=5 --tries=1
--2021-11-30 19:34:57-- http://star-alliance.com/corellian/api
Resolving star-alliance.com (star-alliance.com)... 192.168.64.15
Connecting to star-alliance.com (star-alliance.com)|192.168.64.15|:80... \
connected.
HTTP request sent, awaiting response... 200 OK
...
$ wget star-alliance.com/corellian/api/ --timeout=5 --tries=1
--2021-11-30 15:36:26-- http://star-alliance.com/corellian/api/
Resolving star-alliance.com (star-alliance.com)... 192.168.64.15
Connecting to star-alliance.com (star-alliance.com)|192.168.64.15|:80... \
connected.
HTTP request sent, awaiting response... 404 Not Found
2021-11-30 15:36:26 ERROR 404: Not Found.
```

Using and Configuring CoreDNS

Kubernetes is geared toward operating a microservices architecture. Individual microservices offer distinct, self-contained functionality and communicate with one another to complement each other. Earlier in this chapter, we talked about the usage of a Service to provide a stable network interface. Many of the examples used an IP address and port to talk to a Service.

Kubernetes runs a DNS server implementation called CoreDNS (*https://coredns.io*) that maps the name of the Service to its IP address. In turn, microservices can easily reference the Service name to communicate with each other. For a deep dive on CoreDNS, check out the excellent book *Learning CoreDNS* (O'Reilly).

Inspecting the CoreDNS Pod

The CoreDNS server is running in a Pod in the namespace kube-system. The following command renders the CoreDNS Pod for a Minikube cluster installation:

```
$ kubectl get pods -n kube-system
NAME                         READY   STATUS    RESTARTS   AGE
coredns-558bd4d5db-s89vn     1/1     Running   2          64d
```

CoreDNS uses a so-called Corefile to configure the runtime behavior of the DNS server. The ConfigMap named coredns set up in the same namespace defines the contents of the configuration file. The CoreDNS Pod mounts the ConfigMap, as shown in Example 5-4.

Example 5-4. YAML manifest of CoreDNS Pod

```
apiVersion: v1
kind: Pod
metadata:
  name: coredns-558bd4d5db-s89vn
  namespace: kube-system
...
spec:
  containers:
  - name: coredns
    image: k8s.gcr.io/coredns/coredns:v1.8.0
    volumeMounts:
    - mountPath: /etc/coredns
      name: config-volume
      readOnly: true
  volumes:
  - configMap:
      defaultMode: 420
      items:
      - key: Corefile
        path: Corefile
```

```
      name: coredns
    name: config-volume
...
```

Inspecting the CoreDNS Configuration

You can inspect the ConfigMap with the command `kubectl get configmaps core dns -n kube-system -o yaml`. Example 5-5 shows the content of the `Corefile`. See the CoreDNS manual (*https://oreil.ly/7AeWG*) for more information on the syntax and instructions of a `Corefile`.

Example 5-5. Default Corefile defined by a ConfigMap

```
apiVersion: v1
kind: ConfigMap
metadata:
  name: coredns
  namespace: kube-system
data:
  Corefile: |
    .:53 {
        errors
        health {
           lameduck 5s
        }
        ready
        kubernetes cluster.local in-addr.arpa ip6.arpa {
           pods insecure
           fallthrough in-addr.arpa ip6.arpa
           ttl 30
        }
        prometheus :9153
        hosts {
           192.168.64.1 host.minikube.internal
           fallthrough
        }
        forward . /etc/resolv.conf {
           max_concurrent 1000
        }
        cache 30
        loop
        reload
        loadbalance
    }
...
```

Customizing the CoreDNS Configuration

The default configuration of a `Corefile` can be further customized. To do so, create a new ConfigMap in the namespace `kube-system` in the format shown in Example 5-6.

Example 5-6. Custom Corefile defined by a ConfigMap

```
apiVersion: v1
kind: ConfigMap
metadata:
  name: coredns-custom
  namespace: kube-system
data:
  ...
```

Create the new ConfigMap specified by the file `coredsns-custom.yaml` and force a reload of the CoreDNS Pod configuration by deleting it. The CoreDNS will start up again automatically because the CoreDNS Pod was deployed and managed by the state of the Deployment. The Pod's restart policy defaults to `Always`; deleting the Pod is a quick way to force it to restart, and the new Pod instance will be mapped to the updated information in the ConfigMap:

```
$ kubectl apply -f coredsns-custom.yaml
$ kubectl delete pod coredns -n kube-system
```

DNS for Services

Services tie into the DNS service provided by CoreDNS. In this section, we will talk about various scenarios that illustrate how to talk to a Service from another Pod that lives in the same or a different namespace.

Resolving a Service by Hostname from the Same Namespace

A Pod can resolve the Service by hostname if both objects live in the same namespace. Figure 5-9 illustrates a Pod implementing UI frontend functionality that makes a call to a backend microservice through a Service.

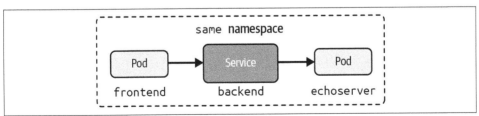

Figure 5-9. Resolving a Service from the same namespace

You can easily verify the behavior with the following commands. Here, we'll create a Service and a Pod in the namespace dns with the name echoserver:

```
$ kubectl create namespace dns
namespace/dns created
$ kubectl run echoserver --image=k8s.gcr.io/echoserver:1.10 --restart=Never \
  --port=8080 --expose -n dns
service/echoserver created
pod/echoserver created
$ kubectl get services,pods -n dns
NAME                  TYPE        CLUSTER-IP      EXTERNAL-IP   PORT(S)    AGE
service/echoserver    ClusterIP   10.99.124.240   <none>        8080/TCP   17m

NAME              READY   STATUS    RESTARTS   AGE
pod/echoserver    1/1     Running   0          17m
```

You can verify the correct service discovery by running a Pod in the same namespace that makes a call to the Service by using its hostname and incoming port:

```
$ kubectl run busybox --image=busybox --rm -it --restart=Never -n dns \
  -- wget echoserver:8080
Connecting to echoserver:8080 (10.99.124.240:8080)
saving to 'index.html'
index.html           100% |********************************|   406  0:00:00 ETA
'index.html' saved
pod "busybox" deleted
```

Resolving a Service by Hostname from a Different Namespace

It's not uncommon to make a call from a Pod to a Service that lives in a different namespace. Referencing just the hostname of the Service does not work across namespaces. You need to append the namespace as well.

Figure 5-10 illustrates a backend Pod in the namespace business that calls a Service in the namespace other. To communicate with the weather-api Service from the namespace business, you will need to reference it via weather-api.other. Services that reside in the default namespace will have to referenced accordingly (e.g., lottery.default).

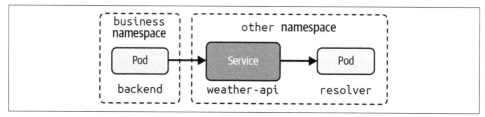

Figure 5-10. Resolving a Service from a different namespace

```
$ kubectl create namespace other
namespace/other created
$ kubectl run echoserver --image=k8s.gcr.io/echoserver:1.10 --restart=Never \
  --port=8080 --expose -n other
service/echoserver created
pod/echoserver created
$ kubectl get services,pods -n other
NAME                       TYPE        CLUSTER-IP      EXTERNAL-IP     PORT(S)     AGE
service/echoserver         ClusterIP   10.99.124.240   <none>          8080/TCP    17m

NAME                   READY     STATUS      RESTARTS    AGE
pod/echoserver         1/1       Running     0           17m
```

From a different namespace, in this case called business, make a call from a
temporary Pod to the Service in the namespace other. Attempting to call the
Service without the namespace results in a failure to connect. You can see in the
following code that the namespace of the Service needs to be spelled out explicitly:
echoserver.other:

```
$ kubectl create namespace business
namespace/business created
$ kubectl run busybox --image=busybox --rm -it --restart=Never -n business \
  -- wget echoserver:8080
wget: bad address 'echoserver:8080'
pod "busybox" deleted
pod other/busybox terminated (Error)
$ kubectl run busybox --image=busybox --rm -it --restart=Never -n business \
  -- wget echoserver.other:8080
Connecting to echoserver.other:8080 (10.99.32.59:8080)
saving to 'index.html'
index.html           100% |******************************|    418  0:00:00 ETA
'index.html' saved
pod "busybox" deleted
```

The Corefile defines a cluster domain. By default, the value of the cluster domain is
cluster.local. You can append the cluster domain to the hostname when referencing a Service. In addition, you'll need to use the type of object you're communicating
with. The string svc describes the type Service. The full hostname for a Service
is echoserver.other.svc.cluster.local. You can see the calls in the following
commands:

```
$ kubectl run busybox --image=busybox --rm -it --restart=Never -n business \
  -- wget echoserver.other.svc:8080
Connecting to echoserver.other.svc:8080 (10.99.32.59:8080)
saving to 'index.html'
index.html           100% |******************************|    426  0:00:00 ETA
'index.html' saved
pod "busybox" deleted
$ kubectl run busybox --image=busybox --rm -it --restart=Never -n business \
  -- wget echoserver.other.svc.cluster.local:8080
Connecting to echoserver.other.svc.cluster.local:8080 (10.99.32.59:8080)
```

```
saving to 'index.html'
index.html          100% |*****************************|   454  0:00:00 ETA
'index.html' saved
pod "busybox" deleted
```

DNS for Pods

Pods can talk to each by IP address across namespaces. CoreDNS provides the configuration option pods insecure in the Corefile file to create DNS records for Pods. To reference a Pod, use the IP address, but replace the dots with dashes. For example, a Pod with the IP address 10.0.0.85 has a corresponding DNS record with 10-0-0-85. Figure 5-11 shows Pods that reference each other by their DNS records.

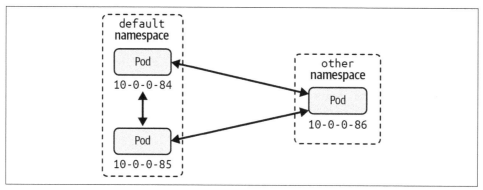

Figure 5-11. Resolving a Pod via DNS records

Resolving a Pod by Hostname

We'll create two Pods to demonstrate the runtime behavior of CoreDNS for Pods. Pod 1, named echoserver1, runs in the namespace ns1 with the IP address 172.17.0.8. Pod 2, named echoserver2, runs in the namespace ns2 with the IP address 172.17.0.9:

```
$ kubectl create namespace ns1
namespace/ns1 created
$ kubectl create namespace ns2
namespace/ns2 created
$ kubectl run echoserver1 --image=k8s.gcr.io/echoserver:1.10 --restart=Never \
  --port=8080 -n ns1
pod/echoserver1 created
$ kubectl run echoserver2 --image=k8s.gcr.io/echoserver:1.10 --restart=Never \
  --port=8080 -n ns2
pod/echoserver2 created
$ kubectl get pod echoserver1 -n ns1 --template={{.status.podIP}}
172.17.0.8
$ kubectl get pod echoserver2 -n ns2 --template={{.status.podIP}}
172.17.0.9
```

For resolving a Pod via DNS, you are required to spell out the namespace and object type as part of the hostname independent of where the Pod lives. The following two commands use a temporary Pod to make a call to another Pod in the same and a different namespace. Adding `cluster.local` is optional:

```
$ kubectl run busybox --image=busybox --rm -it --restart=Never -n ns1 \
  -- wget 172-17-0-8.ns1.pod:8080
Connecting to 172-17-0-8.ns1.pod:8080 (172.17.0.8:8080)
saving to 'index.html'
index.html           100% |*******************************|   424  0:00:00 ETA
'index.html' saved
pod "busybox" deleted
$ kubectl run busybox --image=busybox --rm -it --restart=Never -n ns1 \
  -- wget 172-17-0-9.ns2.pod:8080
Connecting to 172-17-0-9.ns2.pod:8080 (172.17.0.9:8080)
saving to 'index.html'
index.html           100% |*******************************|   424  0:00:00 ETA
'index.html' saved
pod "busybox" deleted
```

This option `pods insecure` exists only for backward compatibility reasons with kube-dns, the original implementation of Kubernetes' DNS server. You can disable the creation of DNS records for Pods by configuring CoreDNS with `pods disabled` instead. It is not recommended to rely on the DNS record for a Pod.

Choosing an Appropriate Container Network Interface Plugin

In Chapter 2, we talked about the mechanics of installing a Container Network Interface plugin. The CNI, a Cloud Native Computing Foundation project, consists of a specification and libraries for writing plugins to configure network interfaces in Linux containers, along with a number of plugins. CNI concerns itself only with network connectivity of containers and removing allocated resources when the container is deleted. Kubernetes uses CNI as an interface between network providers and Kubernetes Pod networking.

The CNI specification defines the Pod networking interface and capabilities. Plugins implement the specification and allow a Kubernetes administrator to pick and choose a product-specific feature set. Figure 5-12 shows a couple of exemplary plugins you can choose from. For a list of plugins, see the Kubernetes documentation (*https:// oreil.ly/mgnMT*).

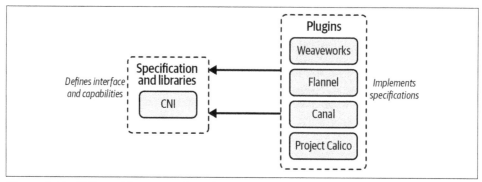

Figure 5-12. CNI specification and implementation

Choosing an appropriate CNI plugin depends on your needs. Refer to this blog post (*https://oreil.ly/8lCIq*) for a decision matrix that can help you make the right choice for your Kubernetes cluster. During the CKA exam, you might be asked to install a CNI plugin. Many of the plugins mentioned in the Kubernetes documentation link to web pages outside of the Kubernetes domain. Remember that you are not allowed to navigate to pages outside of the official Kubernetes documentation during the exam. Take a look at the link in the browser before opening it by hovering over it with the mouse pointer. For example, this Kubernetes documentation section (*https://oreil.ly/ncYMk*) describes the installation instructions for Weave Net.

Summary

Kubernetes assigns a unique IP address for every Pod in the cluster. Pods can communicate with each other using that IP address; however, you cannot rely on the IP address to be stable over time. That's why Kubernetes provides the Service resource type.

A Service forwards network traffic to a set of Pods based on label selection and port mappings. Every Service needs to assign a type that determines how the Service becomes accessible from within or outside of the cluster. The Service types relevant to the CKA exam are ClusterIP, NodePort, and LoadBalancer. CoreDNS, the DNS server for Kubernetes, allows Pods to access the Service by hostname from the same and other namespaces.

The resource type Ingress defines rules for routing incoming, cluster-external HTTP(S) traffic to a Service. An Ingress controller periodically evaluates those rules and ensures that they apply to the cluster.

Exam Essentials

Understand the purpose of a Service
Pod-to-Pod communication via their IP address does'nt guarantee a stable network interface over time. The purpose of a Service is to provide that stable network interface so that you can operate complex microservice architecture that run in a Kubernetes cluster. In most cases, Pods call a Service by hostname. The hostname is provided by CoreDNS.

Practice how to access a Service for each type
The CKA exam expects you to understand the differences between the Service types ClusterIP, NodePort, and LoadBalancer. Depending on the assigned type, a Service becomes accessible from inside the cluster or from outside the cluster.

Understand the difference between a Service and an Ingress
An Ingress is not to be confused with a Service. The Ingress is meant for routing cluster-external HTTP(S) traffic to one or many Services based on an optional hostname and mandatory path. A Service routes traffic to a set of Pods.

Sample Exercises

Solutions to these exercises are available in the Appendix.

1. In the namespace external, create a Deployment named nginx with the image nginx for three replicas. The container should expose the port 80. Within the same namespace, create a Service of type LoadBalancer. The Service should route traffic to the Pods managed by the Deployment.

2. From your local machine (outside the cluster), make a call to the LoadBalancer using wget or curl. Identify which Pods received the traffic by looking at the logs.

3. Change the Service type to ClusterIP. Make a call to the Service using wget or curl so that the Pods receive the traffic.

4. Create an Ingress named incoming in the namespace external. Define the path type Prefix to the path / to the Service from the previous step. The Ingress should be able to handle any incoming HTTP traffic.

5. Make a call to the Ingress using wget or curl from your local machine. Verify that the Pods receive traffic.

6. Create a new Service of type ClusterIP named echoserver in the namespace external. The selected and to-be-created Pod should use the image k8s.gcr.io/echoserver:1.10 on port 8080. Add a new rule to the existing Ingress to route traffic to the echoserver Service with the path /echo and type Exact.

7. Make a call to the Service using `wget` or `curl` from your local machine so that the `echoserver` can be reached.

8. Create a rewrite rule (*https://oreil.ly/ZVYkK*) for the CoreDNS configuration that allows referencing a Service using the cluster domain `cka.example.com`. Ensure that the custom CoreDNS configuration takes effect.

9. Make a call to the `nginx` Service using `wget` or `curl` from a temporary Pod in a new namespace called `hello` with the appropriate hostname.

CHAPTER 6
Storage

When container images are instantiated as containers, the container needs context—context to CPU, memory, and I/O resources. Pods provide the network and the filesystem context for the containers within. The network is provided as the Pod's virtual IP address, and the filesystem is mounted to the hosting node's filesystem. Applications running in the container can interact with the filesystem as part of the Pod context. A container's temporary filesystem is isolated from any other container or Pod and is not persisted beyond a Pod restart. The "Storage" section of the CKA curriculum addresses the technical abstraction in Kubernetes responsible for persisting data beyond a container or Pod restart.

A volume is a Kubernetes capability that persists data beyond a Pod restart. Essentially, a volume is a directory that's shareable between multiple containers of a Pod. You will learn about the different volume types and the process for defining and mounting a volume in a container.

Persistent volumes are a specific category of the wider concept of volumes. The mechanics for persistent volumes are slightly more complex. The persistent volume is the resource that actually persists the data to an underlying physical storage. The persistent volume claim represents the connecting resource between a Pod and a persistent volume responsible for requesting the storage. Finally, the Pod needs to *claim* the persistent volume and mount it to a directory path available to the containers running inside of the Pod.

At a high level, this chapter covers the following concepts:

- Persistent volume
- Static versus dynamic provision of persistent volumes
- Storage Class

- Configuration options for a persistent volume
- Persistent volume claim
- Mounting a persistent volume in a Pod

Understanding Volumes

Applications running in a container can use the temporary filesystem to read and write files. In the case of a container crash or a cluster/node restart, the kubelet will restart the container. Any data that had been written to the temporary filesystem is lost and cannot be retrieved anymore. The container effectively starts with a clean slate again.

There are many uses cases for wanting to mount a volume in a container. One of the most prominent use cases are multi-container Pods (*https://oreil.ly/EtTx4*) that use a volume to exchange data between a main application container and a sidecar. Figure 6-1 illustrates the differences between the temporary filesystem of a container and the use of a volume.

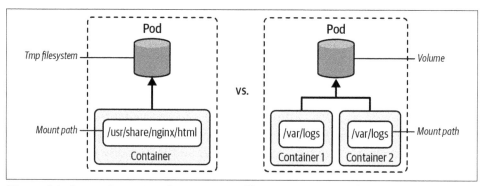

Figure 6-1. A container using the temporary filesystem versus a volume

Volume Types

Every volume needs to define a type. The type determines the medium that backs the volume and its runtime behavior. The Kubernetes documentation offers a long list of volume types. Some of the types—for example, `azureDisk`, `awsElasticBlockStore`, or `gcePersistentDisk`—are available only when running the Kubernetes cluster in a specific cloud provider. Table 6-1 shows a reduced list of volume types that I deem to be most relevant to the exam.

Table 6-1. Volume types relevant to exam

Type	Description
emptyDir	Empty directory in Pod with read/write access. Persisted for only the lifespan of a Pod. A good choice for cache implementations or data exchange between containers of a Pod.
hostPath	File or directory from the host node's filesystem.
configMap, secret	Provides a way to inject configuration data. For practical examples, see "Defining and Consuming Configuration Data" on page 60.
nfs	An existing Network File System (NFS) share. Preserves data after Pod restart.
persistent VolumeClaim	Claims a persistent volume. Fore more information, see "Creating PersistentVolumeClaims" on page 130.

Creating and Accessing Volumes

Defining a volume for a Pod requires two steps. First, you need to declare the volume itself using the attribute `spec.volumes[]`. As part of the definition, you provide the name and the type. Just declaring the volume won't be sufficient, though. Second, the volume needs to be mounted to a path of the consuming container via `spec.containers.volumeMounts[]`. The mapping between the volume and the volume mount occurs by the matching name.

From the YAML manifest stored in the file `pod-with-volume.yaml` and shown in Example 6-1, you can see the definition of a volume with type `emptyDir`. The volume has been mounted to the path */var/logs* inside of the container named `nginx`.

Example 6-1. A Pod defining and mounting a volume

```
apiVersion: v1
kind: Pod
metadata:
  name: business-app
spec:
  volumes:
  - name: logs-volume
    emptyDir: {}
  containers:
  - image: nginx
    name: nginx
    volumeMounts:
    - mountPath: /var/logs
      name: logs-volume
```

Let's create the Pod and see if we can interact with the mounted volume. The following commands open an interactive shell after the Pod's creation and then navigate to the mount path. You can see that the volume type `emptyDir` initializes the mount path as an empty directory. New files and directories can be created as needed without limitations:

```
$ kubectl create -f pod-with-volume.yaml
pod/business-app created
$ kubectl get pod business-app
NAME           READY   STATUS    RESTARTS   AGE
business-app   1/1     Running   0          43s
$ kubectl exec business-app -it -- /bin/sh
# cd /var/logs
# pwd
/var/logs
# ls
# touch app-logs.txt
# ls
app-logs.txt
```

Understanding Persistent Volumes

Data stored on Volumes outlive a container restart. In many applications, the data lives far beyond the lifecycles of the applications, container, Pod, nodes, and even the clusters themselves. Data persistence ensures the lifecycles of the data are decoupled from the lifecycles of the cluster resources. A typical example would be data persisted by a database. That's the responsibility of a persistent volume. Kubernetes models persist data with the help of two primitives: the PersistentVolume and the PersistentVolumeClaim.

The PersistentVolume is the storage device in a Kubernetes cluster. It is completely decoupled from the Pod and therefore has its own lifecycle. The object captures the source of the storage (e.g., storage made available by a cloud provider). A PersistentVolume is either provided by a Kubernetes administrator or assigned dynamically by mapping to a storage class.

The PersistentVolumeClaim requests the resources of a PersistentVolume—for example, the size of the storage and the access type. In the Pod, you will use the type `persistentVolumeClaim` to mount the abstracted PersistentVolume by using the PersistentVolumeClaim.

Figure 6-2 shows the relationship between the Pod, the PersistentVolumeClaim, and the PersistentVolume.

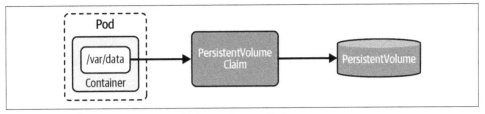

Figure 6-2. Claiming a PersistentVolume from a Pod

Static vs. Dynamic Provisioning

A PersistentVolume can be created statically or dynamically. If you go with the static approach, then you need to create a storage device first and reference it by explicitly creating an object of kind PersistentVolume. The dynamic approach doesn't require you to create a PersistentVolume object. It will be automatically created from the PersistentVolumeClaim by setting a storage class name using the attribute `spec.storageClassName`.

A storage class is an abstraction concept that defines a class of storage device (e.g., storage with slow or fast performance) used for different application types. It's the job of a Kubernetes administrator to set up storage classes. For a deeper discussion on storage classes, see "Understanding Storage Classes" on page 132. For now, we'll focus on the static provisioning of PersistentVolumes.

Creating PersistentVolumes

When you create a PersistentVolume object yourself, we refer to the approach as static provisioning. A PersistentVolume can be created only by using the manifest-first approach. At this time, `kubectl` doesn't allow the creation of a PersistentVolume using the `create` command. Every PersistentVolume needs to define the storage capacity using `spec.capacity` and an access mode set via `spec.accessModes`. See "Configuration Options for a PersistentVolume" on page 128 for more information on the configuration options available to a PersistentVolume.

Example 6-2 creates a PersistentVolume named `db-pv` with a storage capacity of 1Gi and read/write access by a single node. The attribute `hostPath` mounts the directory `/data/db` from the host node's filesystem. We'll store the YAML manifest in the file `db-pv.yaml`.

Example 6-2. YAML manifest defining a PersistentVolume

```
apiVersion: v1
kind: PersistentVolume
metadata:
  name: db-pv
spec:
  capacity:
    storage: 1Gi
  accessModes:
    - ReadWriteOnce
  hostPath:
    path: /data/db
```

Upon inspection of the created PersistentVolume, you'll find most of the information you provided in the manifest. The status `Available` indicates that the object is ready to be claimed. The reclaim policy determines what should happen with the PersistentVolume after it has been released from its claim. By default, the object will be retained. The following example uses the short-form command `pv` to avoid having to type `persistentvolume`:

```
$ kubectl create -f db-pv.yaml
persistentvolume/db-pv created
$ kubectl get pv db-pv
NAME     CAPACITY   ACCESS MODES   RECLAIM POLICY   STATUS      \
   CLAIM   STORAGECLASS   REASON   AGE
db-pv    1Gi        RWO            Retain           Available \
                                   10s
```

Configuration Options for a PersistentVolume

A PersistentVolume offers a variety of configuration options that determine their innate runtime behavior. For the exam, it's important to understand the volume mode, access mode, and reclaim policy configuration options.

Volume Mode

The volume mode handles the type of device. That's a device either meant to be consumed from the filesystem or backed by a block device. The most common case is a filesystem device. You can set the volume mode using the attribute `spec.volumeMode`. Table 6-2 shows all available volume modes.

Table 6-2. PersistentVolume volume modes

Type	Description
Filesystem	Default. Mounts the volume into a directory of the consuming Pod. Creates a filesystem first if the volume is backed by a block device and the device is empty.
Block	Used for a volume as a raw block device without a filesystem on it.

The volume mode is not rendered by default in the console output of the `get pv` command. You will need to provide the `-o wide` command-line option to see the VOLUMEMODE column, as shown here:

```
$ kubectl get pv -o wide
NAME     CAPACITY     ACCESS MODES   RECLAIM POLICY   STATUS     \
CLAIM    STORAGECLASS   REASON   AGE   VOLUMEMODE
db-pv    1Gi          RWO            Retain           Available \
                                19m   Filesystem
```

Access Mode

Each PersistentVolume can express how it can be accessed using the attribute `spec.accessModes`. For example, you can define that the volume can be mounted only by a single Pod in a read or write mode or that a volume is read-only but accessible from different nodes simultaneously. Table 6-3 provides a high-level overview of the available access modes. The short-form notation of the access mode is usually rendered in outputs of specific commands, e.g., `get pv` or `describe pv`.

Table 6-3. PersistentVolume access modes

Type	Short Form	Description
ReadWriteOnce	RWO	Read/write access by a single node
ReadOnlyMany	ROX	Read-only access by many nodes
ReadWriteMany	RWX	Read/write access by many nodes
ReadWriteOncePod	RWOP	Read/write access mounted by a single Pod

The following command parses the access modes from the PersistentVolume named db-pv. As you can see, the returned value is an array underlining the fact that you can assign multiple access modes at once:

```
$ kubectl get pv db-pv -o jsonpath='{.spec.accessModes}'
["ReadWriteOnce"]
```

Reclaim Policy

Optionally, you can also define a reclaim policy for a PersistentVolume. The reclaim policy specifies what should happen to a PersistentVolume object when the bound PersistentVolumeClaim is deleted (see Table 6-4). For dynamically created PersistentVolumes, the reclaim policy can be set via the attribute `.reclaimPolicy` in the storage class. for statically created PersistentVolumes, use the attribute `spec.persistentVolumeReclaimPolicy` in the PersistentVolume definition .

Table 6-4. PersistentVolume reclaim policies

Type	Description
Retain	Default. When PersistentVolumeClaim is deleted, the PersistentVolume is "released" and can be reclaimed.
Delete	Deletion removes PersistentVolume and its associated storage.
Recycle	This value is deprecated. You should use one of the values above.

The following command retrieves the assigned reclaim policy of the PersistentVolume named db-pv:

```
$ kubectl get pv db-pv -o jsonpath='{.spec.persistentVolumeReclaimPolicy}'
Retain
```

Creating PersistentVolumeClaims

The next object we'll need to create is the PersistentVolumeClaim. Its purpose is to bind the PersistentVolume to the Pod. Let's take a look at the YAML manifest stored in the file db-pvc.yaml, as shown in Example 6-3.

Example 6-3. Definition of a PersistentVolumeClaim

```
kind: PersistentVolumeClaim
apiVersion: v1
metadata:
  name: db-pvc
spec:
  accessModes:
    - ReadWriteOnce
  storageClassName: ""
  resources:
    requests:
      storage: 256Mi
```

What we're saying here is, "Give me a PersistentVolume that can fulfill the resource request of 256Mi and provides the access mode ReadWriteOnce." Static provisioning should use an empty string for the attribute spec.storageClassName if you do not want it to automatically assign the default storage class. The binding to an appropriate PersistentVolume happens automatically based on those criteria.

After creating the PersistentVolumeClaim, the status is set as Bound, which means that the binding to the PersistentVolume was successful. Once the associated binding occurs, nothing else can bind to it. The binding relationship is 1-to-1. Nothing else can bind to the PersistentVolume once claimed. The following get command uses the short-form pvc instead of persistentvolumeclaim:

```
$ kubectl create -f db-pvc.yaml
persistentvolumeclaim/db-pvc created
$ kubectl get pvc db-pvc
NAME      STATUS   VOLUME   CAPACITY   ACCESS MODES   STORAGECLASS   AGE
db-pvc    Bound    db-pv    1Gi        RWO                           111s
```

The PersistentVolume has not been mounted by a Pod yet. Therefore, inspecting the details of the object shows <none>. Using the describe command is a good way to verify if the PersistentVolumeClaim was mounted properly:

```
$ kubectl describe pvc db-pvc
...
Used By:        <none>
...
```

Mounting PersistentVolumeClaims in a Pod

All that's left is to mount the PersistentVolumeClaim in the Pod that wants to consume it. You already learned how to mount a volume in a Pod. The big difference here shown in Example 6-4 is using spec.volumes[].persistentVolumeClaim and providing the name of the PersistentVolumeClaim.

Example 6-4. A Pod referencing a PersistentVolumeClaim

```yaml
apiVersion: v1
kind: Pod
metadata:
  name: app-consuming-pvc
spec:
  volumes:
    - name: app-storage
      persistentVolumeClaim:
        claimName: db-pvc
  containers:
  - image: alpine
    name: app
    command: ["/bin/sh"]
    args: ["-c", "while true; do sleep 60; done;"]
    volumeMounts:
      - mountPath: "/mnt/data"
        name: app-storage
```

Let's assume we stored the configuration in the file `app-consuming-pvc.yaml`. After creating the Pod from the manifest, you should see the Pod transitioning into the Ready state. The `describe` command will provide additional information on the volume:

```
$ kubectl create -f app-consuming-pvc.yaml
pod/app-consuming-pvc created
$ kubectl get pods
NAME                   READY   STATUS    RESTARTS   AGE
app-consuming-pvc      1/1     Running   0          3s
$ kubectl describe pod app-consuming-pvc
...
Volumes:
  app-storage:
    Type:       PersistentVolumeClaim (a reference to a PersistentVolumeClaim \
                in the same namespace)
    ClaimName:  db-pvc
    ReadOnly:   false
...
```

The PersistentVolumeClaim now also shows the Pod that mounted it:

```
$ kubectl describe pvc db-pvc
...
Used By:        app-consuming-pvc
...
```

You can now go ahead and open an interactive shell to the Pod. Navigating to the mount path at */mnt/data* gives you access to the underlying PersistentVolume:

```
$ kubectl exec app-consuming-pvc -it -- /bin/sh
/ # cd /mnt/data
/mnt/data # ls -l
total 0
/mnt/data # touch test.db
/mnt/data # ls -l
total 0
-rw-r--r--    1 root     root             0 Sep 29 23:59 test.db
```

Understanding Storage Classes

A storage class is a Kubernetes primitive that defines a specific type or "class" of storage. Typical characteristics of a storage can be the type (e.g., fast SSD storage versus a remote cloud storage or the backup policy for a storage). The storage class is used to provision a PersistentVolume dynamically based on its criteria. In practice, this means that you do not have to create the PersistentVolume object yourself. The provisioner assigned to the storage class takes care of it. Most Kubernetes cloud providers come with a list of existing provisioners. Minikube already creates a default storage class named `standard`, which you can query for with the following command:

```
$ kubectl get storageclass
NAME                    PROVISIONER                 RECLAIMPOLICY \
  VOLUMEBINDINGMODE     ALLOWVOLUMEEXPANSION  AGE
standard (default)      k8s.io/minikube-hostpath    Delete        \
  Immediate             false                 108d
```

Creating Storage Classes

Storage classes can be created declaratively only with the help of a YAML manifest. At a minimum, you need to declare the provisioner. All other attributes are optional and use default values if not provided upon creation. Most provisioners let you set parameters specific to the storage type. Example 6-5 defines a storage class on Google Compute Engine denoted by the provisioner kubernetes.io/gce-pd.

Example 6-5. Definition of a storage class

```
apiVersion: storage.k8s.io/v1
kind: StorageClass
metadata:
  name: fast
provisioner: kubernetes.io/gce-pd
parameters:
  type: pd-ssd
  replication-type: regional-pd
```

Say you saved the YAML contents in the file fast-sc.yaml; then the following command will create the object. The storage class can be listed using the get storage class command:

```
$ kubectl create -f fast-sc.yaml
storageclass.storage.k8s.io/fast created
$ kubectl get storageclass
NAME                    PROVISIONER                 RECLAIMPOLICY \
  VOLUMEBINDINGMODE     ALLOWVOLUMEEXPANSION  AGE
fast                    kubernetes.io/gce-pd        Delete        \
  Immediate             false                 4s
...
```

Using Storage Classes

Provisioning a PersistentVolume dynamically requires the assignment of the storage class when you create the PeristentVolumeClaim. Example 6-6 shows the usage of the attribute spec.storageClassName for assigning the storage class named standard.

Example 6-6. Using a storage class in a PersistentVolumeClaim

```
kind: PersistentVolumeClaim
apiVersion: v1
metadata:
  name: db-pvc
spec:
  accessModes:
    - ReadWriteOnce
  resources:
    requests:
      storage: 512Mi
  storageClassName: standard
```

The corresponding PersistentVolume object will be created only if the storage class can provision a fitting PersistentVolume using its provisioner. It's important to understand that Kubernetes does not render an error or warning message if it isn't the case.

The following command renders the created PersistentVolumeClaim and Persistent-Volume. As you can see, the name of the dynamically provisioned PersistentVolume is using a hash to ensure a unique naming:

```
$ kubectl get pv,pvc
NAME                                                         CAPACITY \
  ACCESS MODES  RECLAIM POLICY  STATUS  CLAIM          STORAGECLASS \
  REASON  AGE
persistentvolume/pvc-b820b919-f7f7-4c74-9212-ef259d421734   512Mi \
    RWO           Delete          Bound   default/db-pvc standard \
                  2s

NAME                          STATUS  VOLUME                                  \
CAPACITY  ACCESS MODES  STORAGECLASS  AGE
persistentvolumeclaim/db-pvc  Bound   pvc-b820b919-f7f7-4c74-9212-ef259d421734 \
512Mi     RWO           standard      2s
```

The steps for mounting the PersistentVolumeClaim from a Pod are the same as for static and dynamic provisioning. Refer to "Mounting PersistentVolumeClaims in a Pod" on page 131 for more information.

Summary

Containers store data in a temporary filesystem, which is empty each time a new Pod is started. Application developers need to persist data beyond the lifecycles of the containers, Pods, node, and cluster. Typical examples include persistent log files or data in a database.

Kubernetes offers the concept of a volume to implement the use case. A Pod mounts a volume to a path in the container. Any data written to the mounted storage will be persisted beyond a container restart. Kubernetes offers a wide range of volume types to fulfill different requirements.

PersistentVolumes even store data beyond a Pod or cluster/node restart. Those objects are decoupled from the Pod's lifecycle and are therefore represented by a Kubernetes primitive. The PersistentVolumeClaim abstracts the underlying implementation details of a PersistentVolume and acts as an intermediary between the Pod and PersistentVolume. A PersistentVolume can be provisioned statically by creating the object or dynamically with the help of a provisioner assigned to a storage class.

Exam Essentials

Understand the need and use cases for a volume

Many production-ready application stacks running in a cloud-native environment need to persist data. Read up on common use cases and explore recipes that describe typical scenarios. You can find some examples in the O'Reilly books *Kubernetes Patterns, Kubernetes Best Practices*, and *Cloud Native DevOps with Kubernetes*.

Practice defining and consuming volumes

Volumes are a cross-cutting concept applied in different areas of the exam. Know where to find the relevant documentation for defining a volume and the multitude of ways to consume a volume from a container. Definitely revisit "Defining and Consuming Configuration Data" on page 60 for a deep dive on how to mount ConfigMaps and Secrets as a volume.

Internalize the mechanics of defining and consuming a PersistentVolume

Creating a PersistentVolume involves a couple of moving parts. Understand the configuration options for PersistentVolumes and PersistentVolumeClaims and how they play together. Try to emulate situations that prevent a successful binding of a PersistentVolumeClaim. Then fix the situation by taking counteractions. Internalize the short-form commands pv and pvc to save precious time during the exam.

Know the differences between static and dynamic provisioning of a PersistentVolume

A PersistentVolume can be created statically by creating the object from a YAML manifest using the create command. Alternatively, you can let Kubernetes provision a PersistentVolume dynamically without your direct involvement. For this to happen, assign a storage class to the PersistentVolumeClaim. The provisioner of the storage class takes care of creating PersistentVolume object for you.

Sample Exercises

Solutions to these exercises are available in the Appendix.

1. Create a PersistentVolume named logs-pv that maps to the hostPath *ered/tmp/logs*. The access mode should be ReadWriteOnce and ReadOnlyMany. Provision a storage capacity of 2Gi. Assign the reclaim policy Delete and an empty string as the storage class. Ensure that the status of the PersistentVolume shows Available.

2. Create a PersistentVolumeClaim named logs-pvc. The access it uses is ReadWriteOnce. Request a capacity of 1Gi. Ensure that the status of the PersistentVolume shows Bound.

3. Mount the PersistentVolumeClaim in a Pod running the image nginx at the mount path */var/log/nginx*.

4. Open an interactive shell to the container and create a new file named *my-nginx.log* in */var/log/nginx*. Exit out of the Pod.

5. Delete the Pod and PersistentVolumeClaim. What happens to the PersistentVolume?

6. List the available storage classes and identify the default storage class. Note the provisioner.

7. Create a new storage class named custom using the provisioner of the default storage class.

8. Create a PersistentVolumeClaim named custom-pvc. Request a capacity of 500Mi and declare the access mode ReadWriteOnce. Assign the storage class name custom.

9. The PersistentVolume should have been provisioned dynamically. Find out the name and write it to the file named pv-name.txt.

10. Delete the PersistentVolumeClaim. What happens to the PersistentVolume?

## CHAPTER 7

Troubleshooting

Establishing a Kubernetes cluster is one thing. Making sure that the cluster stays operational is another. As a Kubernetes administrator, you are continuously confronted with making sure that the cluster stays functional. Therefore, your troubleshooting skills must be sharp so that you can come up with strategies for identifying the root cause of an issue and fixing it.

Of all the domains covered by the exam, the section "Troubleshooting" has the highest weight for the overall score, so it's important to understand failure scenarios and learn how to fix them. This chapter will address how to monitor and troubleshoot applications in different constellations. Furthermore, we'll discuss failures that may arise for cluster components due to misconfiguration or error conditions.

At a high level, this chapter covers the following concepts:

- Evaluating logging options
- Monitoring applications
- Accessing container logs
- Troubleshooting application failures
- Troubleshooting cluster failures

Evaluating Cluster and Node Logging

A real-world Kubernetes cluster manages hundreds or even thousands of Pods. For every Pod, you have at least a single container running a process. Each process can produce log output to the standard output or standard error streams. It's imperative to capture the log output to proficiently determine the root cause of an application error. Moreover, cluster components produce logs for diagnostic purposes.

As you can see, Kubernetes' logging mechanism is crucial for tracking down errors and monitoring cluster components and applications. Kubernetes can be configured to log on the cluster or the node level. The implementation approaches and their potential trade-offs may differ from one another.

Cluster Logging

Kubernetes doesn't provide a native solution for cluster-level logging, but you can choose from the following three options to fulfill the requirements:

- Instantiating a node-level logging agent that runs on each of the cluster nodes
- Configuring a sidecar container responsible for handling the application logs
- Pushing the logs directly to a logging backend from the application logic

The following discussion explains the benefits and drawbacks for each approach. For a detailed discussion, see the Kubernetes documentation (*https://oreil.ly/rJjfV*).

Using a node logging agent

The logging agent is a dedicated tool that publishes the logs to a backend. A backend can be an external logging service outside of the cluster. Figure 7-1 visualizes the logging architecture.

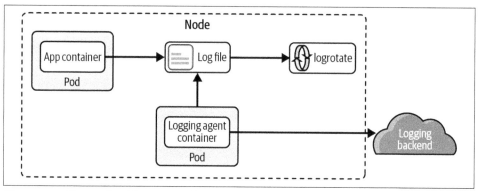

Figure 7-1. Cluster-level logging with an agent

The benefit of this approach is that the application doesn't require any changes to the code or the Pod configuration to support collecting logs. Agents should be run as a DaemonSet.

Using a sidecar container

A Pod can be configured to run another sidecar container alongside the main application container. The sidecar container streams standard output and error produced by the application and redirects the streams to a different location (e.g., a logging backend or a volume mounted to the container). Figure 7-2 shows the logging setup of a Pod that incorporates a streaming sidecar.

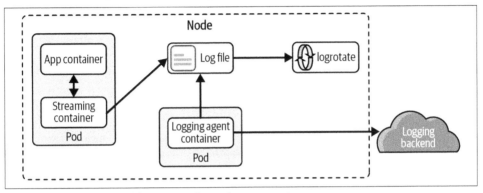

Figure 7-2. Cluster-level logging with a sidecar container

This approach has the benefit of being able to easily separate different streams (e.g., separating error from info log entries).

Pushing directly to logging backend

This approach pushes the responsibility onto the application without adding a middleman. Figure 7-3 shows the logging setup.

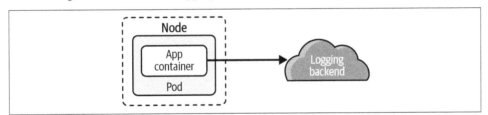

Figure 7-3. Cluster-level logging by directly pushing to the backend

While architecturally less complex, any change to the logging backend will require a change to the application code and therefore a new deployment.

Node Logging

Node logging comes with the implication that the log files will be stored on the cluster node. The container runtime (e.g., Docker Engine) redirects standard output and error streams to the storage of the node with the help of the configured logging driver.

To avoid filling up the node storage with logging content, log rotation should be implemented. Log rotation is an automated process for compressing, moving, deleting, and/or archiving log data that grow beyond a certain threshold. The Linux tool logrotate (*https://oreil.ly/DE7XB*) is one way to configure log rotation for a Kubernetes cluster. Figure 7-4 visualizes the node-level architecture.

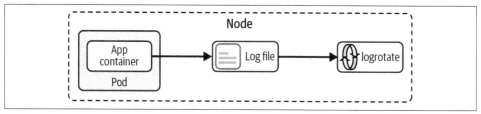

Figure 7-4. Node-level logging

When you run kubectl logs, the kubelet receives the request, reads directly from the log file on the node, and returns the content to the client. The kubectl logs command returns only the latest log content, not the log entries that have already been archived.

The cluster components kube-scheduler and kube-proxy run in a container. Therefore, the log handling is the same as for any other application container. For system components that do not run in the container (e.g., the kubelet and the container runtime), logs will be written to journald if systemd is available. If systemd is not available, system components write their log files to the directory /var/log with the file extension .log.

Monitoring Cluster Components and Applications

Deploying software to a Kubernetes cluster is only the start of operating an application long-term. Developers and administrators alike need to understand resource consumption patterns and behaviors of their applications with the goal of providing a scalable and reliable service.

In the Kubernetes world, monitoring tools like Prometheus and Datadog help with collecting, processing, and visualizing the information over time. The exam does not expect you to be familiar with commercial monitoring, logging, tracing, and aggregation tools; however, it is helpful to gain a rough understanding of the underlying

Kubernetes infrastructure responsible for collecting usage metrics. The following list shows examples of typical metrics:

- Number of nodes in the cluster
- Health status of nodes
- Node performance metrics such as CPU, memory, disk space, network
- Pod-level performance metrics such as CPU and memory consumption

This responsibility falls into the hands of the metrics server (*https://oreil.ly/OycST*), a cluster-wide aggregator of resource usage data. As shown in Figure 7-5, kubelets running on nodes collect the metrics and send them to the metrics server.

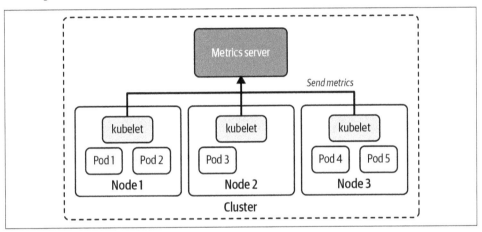

Figure 7-5. Data collection for the metrics server

The metrics server stores data in memory and does not persist data over time. If you are looking for a solution that keeps historical data, then you need to look into commercial options. Refer to the documentation for more information on its installation process. If you're using Minikube as your practice environment, enabling the metrics-server add-on (*https://oreil.ly/NanXK*) is straightforward using the following command:

```
$ minikube addons enable metrics-server
The 'metrics-server' addon is enabled
```

You can now query for metrics of cluster nodes and Pods with the top command:

```
$ kubectl top nodes
NAME        CPU(cores)   CPU%    MEMORY(bytes)   MEMORY%
minikube    283m         14%     1262Mi          32%
$ kubectl top pod frontend
NAME        CPU(cores)   MEMORY(bytes)
frontend    0m           2Mi
```

Troubleshooting Application Failures

When operating an application in a production Kubernetes cluster, it's almost inevitable that you'll come across failure situations. It's your responsibility as an administrator (potentially working closely with the application developer) to troubleshoot issues with deployed Kubernetes objects.

In this section, we're going to take a look at debugging strategies that can help with identifying the root cause of an issue so that you can take action and correct the failure appropriately. For more information, reference the Kubernetes documentation (*https://oreil.ly/4pxVS*).

Troubleshooting Pods

In most cases, creating a Pod is no issue. You simply emit the `run`, `create`, or `apply` commands to instantiate the Pod. If the YAML manifest is formed properly, Kubernetes accepts your request, so the assumption is that everything works as expected. To verify the correct behavior, the first thing you'll want to do is to check the high-level runtime information of the Pod. The operation could involve other Kubernetes objects like a Deployment responsible for rolling out multiple replicas of a Pod.

Retrieving high-level information

To retrieve the information, run either the `kubectl get pods` command for just the Pods running in the namespace or the `kubectl get all` command to retrieve the most prominent object types in the namespace (which includes Deployments). You will want to take a look at the columns `READY`, `STATUS`, and `RESTARTS`. In the optimal case, the number of ready containers matches the number of containers expected to be created by the Pod. For a single-container Pod, the `READY` column would say 1/1. The status should say `Running` to indicate that the Pod entered the proper lifecycle state. Be aware that it's totally possible that a Pod renders a `Running` state, but the application isn't actually working properly. If the number of restarts is greater than 0, then you might want to check the logic of the liveness probe (if defined) and identify the reason why a restart was necessary.

The following Pod observes the status `ErrImagePull` and makes 0/1 containers available to incoming traffic. In short, this Pod has a problem:

```
$ kubectl get pods
NAME                  READY   STATUS        RESTARTS   AGE
pod/misbehaving-pod   0/1     ErrImagePull  0          2s
```

After working with Kubernetes for a while, you'll automatically recognize common error conditions. Table 7-1 lists some of those error statuses and explains how to fix them.

Table 7-1. Common Pod error statuses

Status	Root cause	Potential fix
`ImagePullBackOff` or `ErrImagePull`	Image could not be pulled from registry.	Check correct image name, check that image name exists in registry, verify network access from node to registry, ensure proper authentication.
`CrashLoopBackOff`	Application or command run in container crashes.	Check command executed in container, ensure that image can properly execute (e.g., by creating a container with Docker).
`CreateContainerCon figError`	ConfigMap or Secret referenced by container cannot be found.	Check correct name of the configuration object, verify the existence of the configuration object in the namespace.

Inspecting events

It's totally possible that you'll not encounter any of those error statuses. But there's still a chance of the Pod having a configuration issue. You can retrieve detailed information about the Pod and its events using the kubectl describe pod command to inspect its events. The following output belongs to a Pod that tries to mount a Secret that doesn't exist. Instead of rendering a specific error message, the Pod gets stuck with the status ContainerCreating:

```
$ kubectl get pods
NAME          READY   STATUS             RESTARTS   AGE
secret-pod    0/1     ContainerCreating  0          4m57s
$ kubectl describe pod secret-pod
...
Events:
  Type     Reason       Age                     From                  Message
  ----     ------       ----                    ----                  -------
  Normal   Scheduled    <unknown>               default-scheduler \
  Successfully assigned default/secret-pod to minikube
  Warning  FailedMount  3m15s                   kubelet, minikube  Unable to \
  attach or mount volumes: unmounted volumes=[mysecret], unattached \
  volumes=[default-token-bf8rh mysecret]: timed out waiting for the condition
  Warning  FailedMount  68s (x10 over 5m18s)  kubelet, minikube  \
  MountVolume.SetUp failed for volume "mysecret" : secret "mysecret" not found
  Warning  FailedMount  61s                     kubelet, minikube  Unable to \
  attach or mount volumes: unmounted volumes=[mysecret], unattached \
  volumes=[mysecret default-token-bf8rh]: timed out waiting for the condition
```

Another helpful command is kubectl get events. The output of the command lists the events across all Pods for a given namespace. You can use additional command-line options to further filter and sort events:

```
$ kubectl get events
LAST SEEN   TYPE      REASON           OBJECT              MESSAGE
3m14s       Warning   BackOff          pod/custom-cmd      Back-off \
restarting failed container
2s          Warning   FailedNeedsStart cronjob/google-ping Cannot \
```

```
determine if job needs to be started: too many missed start time (> 100). \
Set or decrease .spec.startingDeadlineSeconds or check clock skew
```

Inspecting logs

When debugging a Pod, the next level of details can be retrieved by downloading and inspecting its logs. You may or may not find additional information that points to the root cause of a misbehaving Pod. It's definitely worth a look. The YAML manifest shown in Example 7-1 defines a Pod running a shell command.

Example 7-1. A Pod running a failing shell command

```
apiVersion: v1
kind: Pod
metadata:
  name: incorrect-cmd-pod
spec:
  containers:
  - name: test-container
    image: busybox
    command: ["/bin/sh", "-c", "unknown"]
```

After creating the object, the Pod fails with the status `CrashLoopBackOff`. Running the `logs` command reveals that the command run in the container has an issue:

```
$ kubectl create -f crash-loop-backoff.yaml
pod/incorrect-cmd-pod created
$ kubectl get pods incorrect-cmd-pod
NAME                READY   STATUS           RESTARTS   AGE
incorrect-cmd-pod   0/1     CrashLoopBackOff  5          3m20s
$ kubectl logs incorrect-cmd-pod
/bin/sh: unknown: not found
```

The `logs` command provides two helpful options I'd like to mention here. The option `-f` streams the logs, meaning you'll see new log entries as they're being produced in real time. The option `--previous` gets the logs from the previous instantiation of a container, which is helpful if the container has been restarted.

Opening an Interactive Shell

If any of the previous commands do not point you to the root cause of the failing Pod, it's time to open an interactive shell to a container. As an application developer, you'll probably know best what behavior to expect from the application at runtime. Ensure that the correct configuration has been created and inspect the running processes by using the Unix or Windows utility tools, depending on the image run in the container.

Say you encounter a situation where a Pod seems to work properly on the surface, as shown in Example 7-2.

Example 7-2. A Pod periodically writing the current date to a file

```
apiVersion: v1
kind: Pod
metadata:
  name: failing-pod
spec:
  containers:
  - args:
    - /bin/sh
    - -c
    - while true; do echo $(date) >> ~/tmp/curr-date.txt; sleep \
      5; done;
    image: busybox
    name: failing-pod
```

After creating the Pod, you check the status. It says Running; however, when making a request to the application, the endpoint reports an error. Next, you check the logs. The log output renders an error message that points to a nonexistent directory. Apparently, the directory hasn't been set up correctly but is needed by the application:

```
$ kubectl create -f failing-pod.yaml
pod/failing-pod created
$ kubectl get pods failing-pod
NAME          READY   STATUS    RESTARTS   AGE
failing-pod   1/1     Running   0          5s
$ kubectl logs failing-pod
/bin/sh: can't create /root/tmp/curr-date.txt: nonexistent directory
```

The exec command opens an interactive shell to further investigate the issue. Below, we're using the Unix tools mkdir, cd, and ls inside of the running container to fix the problem. Obviously, the better mitigation strategy is to create the directory from the application or provide an instruction in the Dockerfile:

```
$ kubectl exec failing-pod -it -- /bin/sh
# mkdir -p ~/tmp
# cd ~/tmp
# ls -l
total 4
-rw-r--r-- 1 root root 112 May  9 23:52 curr-date.txt
```

Troubleshooting Services

A Service provides a unified network interface for Pods. For full coverage on networking aspects in Kubernetes, see Chapter 5. Here, I want to point out troubleshooting techniques for this primitive.

In case you can't reach the Pods that should map to the Service, start by ensuring that the label selector matches with the assigned labels of the Pods. You can query the information by describing the Service and then render the labels of the available Pods with the option `--show-labels`. The following example does not have matching labels and therefore wouldn't apply to any of the Pods running in the namespace:

```
$ kubectl describe service myservice
...
Selector:          app=myapp
...
$ kubectl get pods --show-labels
NAME                        READY   STATUS    RESTARTS   AGE     LABELS
myapp-68bf896d89-qfhlv      1/1     Running   0          7m39s   app=hello
myapp-68bf896d89-tzt55      1/1     Running   0          7m37s   app=world
```

Alternatively, you can also query the endpoints of the Service instance. Say you expected three Pods to be selected by a matching label but only two have been exposed by the Service. You'll want to look at the label selection criteria:

```
$ kubectl get endpoints myservice
NAME        ENDPOINTS                        AGE
myservice   172.17.0.5:80,172.17.0.6:80      9m31s
```

A common source of confusion is the type of a Service. By default, the Service type is `ClusterIP`, which means that a Pod can be reached through the Service only if queried from the same node inside of the cluster. First, check the Service type. If you think that `ClusterIP` is the proper type you wanted to assign, open an interactive shell from a temporary Pod inside the cluster and run a `curl` or `wget` command:

```
$ kubectl get services
NAME        TYPE         CLUSTER-IP      EXTERNAL-IP   PORT(S)   AGE
myservice   ClusterIP    10.99.155.165   <none>        80/TCP    15m
$ kubectl run tmp --image=busybox -it --rm -- wget -O- 10.99.155.165:80
...
```

Finally, check if the port mapping from the target port of the Service to the container port of the Pod is configured correctly. Both ports need to match or the network traffic wouldn't be routed properly:

```
$ kubectl get service myapp -o yaml | grep targetPort:
    targetPort: 80
$ kubectl get pods myapp-68bf896d89-qfhlv -o yaml | grep containerPort:
    - containerPort: 80
```

Troubleshooting Cluster Failures

There are many influencing factors that can render a Kubernetes cluster faulty on the component level. It's a good idea to list the nodes available in the cluster to identify potential issues:

```
$ kubectl get nodes
NAME           STATUS   ROLES                   AGE     VERSION
minikube       Ready    control-plane,master    3m18s   v1.22.3
minikube-m02   Ready    <none>                  2m51s   v1.22.3
minikube-m03   Ready    <none>                  2m24s   v1.22.3
```

The output will give you a lay of the land. You can easily identify the responsibility of each node from the ROLES column, the Kubernetes version used, and the current health status.

There are a couple of things to look out for when identifying issues at a high level:

- Is the health status for the node anything other than "Ready"?
- Does the version of a node deviate from the version of other nodes?

In the following sections you can find individual sections on troubleshooting control plane nodes versus worker nodes.

Troubleshooting Control Plane Nodes

Control plane nodes are the critical components for keeping a cluster operational. As described in "Managing a Highly Available Cluster" on page 31, a cluster can consist of more than one control plane node to ensure a high degree of uptime. Detecting that one of the control plane nodes is faulty should be treated with extreme urgency to avoid compromising high-availability characteristics. For more information on troubleshooting techniques and root-cause analysis, reference the Kubernetes documentation (*https://oreil.ly/KWeTt*).

Rendering cluster information

To further diagnose issues on the control plane node, run the command kubectl cluster-info. As you can see in the following output, the command renders the addresses of the control plane and other cluster services:

```
$ kubectl cluster-info
Kubernetes control plane is running at https://192.168.64.21:8443
CoreDNS is running at https://192.168.64.21:8443/api/v1/namespaces/ \
kube-system/services/kube-dns:dns/proxy

To further debug and diagnose cluster problems, use kubectl cluster-info dump.
```

For a detailed view of the cluster logs, append the dump subcommand. Due to the pages and pages of log messages, we won't render the output in this book. Parse through the message to see if you can find any errors:

```
$ kubectl cluster-info dump
```

Inspecting control plane components

Among those components available on the control plane node (*https://oreil.ly/IZR8Z*) are the following:

- kube-apiserver: Exposes the Kubernetes API used by clients like `kubectl` for managing objects.
- etcd: A key-value store for storing the cluster data.
- kube-scheduler: Selects nodes for Pods that have been scheduled but not created.
- kube-controller-manager: Runs controller processes (e.g., the job controller responsible for Job object execution).
- cloud-controller-manager: Links cloud provider–specific API to the Kubernetes cluster. This controller is not available in on-premise cluster installations of Kubernetes.

To discover those components and their status, list the Pods available in the namespace `kube-system`. Here, you can find the list of control-plane components on Minikube:

```
$ kubectl get pods -n kube-system
NAME                              READY   STATUS    RESTARTS       AGE
etcd-minikube                     1/1     Running   1 (11d ago)    29d
kube-apiserver-minikube           1/1     Running   1 (11d ago)    29d
kube-controller-manager-minikube  1/1     Running   1 (11d ago)    29d
kube-scheduler-minikube           1/1     Running   1 (11d ago)    29d
...
```

Any status that does not show "Running" should be inspected further. You can retrieve the logs for control-plane component Pods in the same fashion you do for any other Pod, using the `logs` command. The following command downloads the logs for the kube-apiserver component:

```
$ kubectl logs kube-apiserver-minikube -n kube-system
```

Troubleshooting Worker Nodes

Worker nodes are responsible for managing the workload. Make sure you have a sufficient number of worker nodes available to distribute the load. For a deeper discussion on how to join worker nodes to a cluster, see Chapter 2.

Any of the nodes available in a cluster can transition into an error state. It's your job as a Kubernetes administrator to identify those situations and fix them in a timely manner. When listing the nodes of a cluster, you may see that a worker node is not in the "Ready" state, which is a good indicator that it's not available to handle the workload. In the output of the `get nodes` command, you can see that the node named `worker-1` is in the "NotReady" state:

```
$ kubectl get nodes
NAME              STATUS    ROLES                  AGE     VERSION
k8s-control-plane Ready     control-plane,master   4d20h   v1.22.3
worker-1          NotReady  <none>                 4d20h   v1.22.3
worker-2          Ready     <none>                 4d20h   v1.22.3
```

The "NotReady" state means that the node is unused and will accumulate operational costs without actually scheduling workload. There might be a variety of reasons why the node entered this state. The following list shows the most common reasons:

- Insufficient resources: The node may be low on memory or disk space.

- Issues with the kubelet process: The process may have crashed or stopped on the node. Therefore, it cannot communicate with the API server running on any of the control plane nodes anymore.

- Issues with kube-proxy: The Pod running kube-proxy is responsible for network communication from within the cluster and from the outside. The Pod transitioned into a nonfunctional state.

SSH into the relevant worker node(s) and start your investigation.

Checking available resources

A good way to identify the root cause of an unavailable worker node is to look at its details. The describe node command renders the section labeled "Conditions":

```
$ kubectl describe node worker-1
....
Conditions:
  Type               Status  LastHeartbeatTime                 \
    LastTransitionTime              Reason                     Message
  ----               ------  -----------------                 \
    -----------------               ------                     -------
  NetworkUnavailable False   Thu, 20 Jan 2022 18:12:13 +0000 \
    Thu, 20 Jan 2022 18:12:13 +0000  CalicoIsUp                \
        Calico is running on this node
  MemoryPressure     False   Tue, 25 Jan 2022 15:59:18 +0000 \
    Thu, 20 Jan 2022 18:11:47 +0000  KubeletHasSufficientMemory \
      kubelet has sufficient memory available
  DiskPressure       False   Tue, 25 Jan 2022 15:59:18 +0000 \
    Thu, 20 Jan 2022 18:11:47 +0000  KubeletHasNoDiskPressure \
        kubelet has no disk pressure
  PIDPressure        False   Tue, 25 Jan 2022 15:59:18 +0000 \
    Thu, 20 Jan 2022 18:11:47 +0000  KubeletHasSufficientPID  \
        kubelet has sufficient PID available
  Ready              True    Tue, 25 Jan 2022 15:59:18 +0000 \
    Thu, 20 Jan 2022 18:12:07 +0000  KubeletReady             \
        kubelet is posting ready status. AppArmor enabled
  ...
```

The table contains information about the resources available to the node, as well as an indication of other services like networking. See if any of the resource types render the status `True` or `Unknown`, which means that there's an issue with the particular resource. You can further troubleshoot unavailable resources with a system-level command.

To check on memory and the number of processes running, use the `top` command:

```
$ top
top - 18:45:09 up 1 day,  2:21,  1 user,  load average: 0.13, 0.13, 0.15
Tasks: 116 total,   3 running,  70 sleeping,   0 stopped,   0 zombie
%Cpu(s):  1.5 us,  0.8 sy,  0.0 ni, 97.7 id,  0.0 wa,  0.0 hi,  0.0 si,  0.0 st
KiB Mem :  1008552 total,   134660 free,   264604 used,   609288 buff/cache
KiB Swap:        0 total,        0 free,        0 used.   611248 avail Mem
...
```

To check on the available disk space, use the command `df`:

```
$ df -h
Filesystem      Size  Used Avail Use% Mounted on
udev            480M     0  480M   0% /dev
tmpfs            99M  1.0M   98M   2% /run
/dev/sda1        39G  2.7G   37G   7% /
tmpfs           493M     0  493M   0% /dev/shm
tmpfs           5.0M     0  5.0M   0% /run/lock
tmpfs           493M     0  493M   0% /sys/fs/cgroup
vagrant         1.9T  252G  1.6T  14% /vagrant
tmpfs            99M     0   99M   0% /run/user/1000
```

Checking the kubelet process

Some conditions rendered by the `describe node` command mention the kubelet process. If you look at the `Message` column, you might get an idea if the kubelet process is running properly. To troubleshoot a misbehaving kubelet process, run the following `systemctl` command:

```
$ systemctl status kubelet
● kubelet.service - kubelet: The Kubernetes Node Agent
   Loaded: loaded (/lib/systemd/system/kubelet.service; enabled; \
   vendor preset: enabled)
  Drop-In: /etc/systemd/system/kubelet.service.d
           └─10-kubeadm.conf
   Active: active (running) since Thu 2022-01-20 18:11:41 UTC; 5 days ago
     Docs: https://kubernetes.io/docs/home/
 Main PID: 6537 (kubelet)
    Tasks: 15 (limit: 1151)
   CGroup: /system.slice/kubelet.service
           └─6537 /usr/bin/kubelet \
             --bootstrap-kubeconfig=/etc/kubernetes/bootstrap-kubelet.conf \
             --kubeconfig=/etc/kubernetes/kubelet.conf \
             --config=/var/lib/kubelet/config.yaml --network-lines 1-10/10
```

The most important information in the output is the value of the `Active` attribute. If it says something other than "active (running)," then you will need to dig deeper. Use `journalctl` to take a look at the log files of the process:

```
$ journalctl -u kubelet.service
-- Logs begin at Thu 2022-01-20 18:10:41 UTC, end at
Tue 2022-01-25 18:44:05 UTC. --
Jan 20 18:11:31 worker-1 systemd[1]: Started kubelet: The Kubernetes Node Agent.
Jan 20 18:11:31 worker-1 systemd[1]: kubelet.service: Current command vanished \
from the unit file, execution of the command list won't be resumed.
Jan 20 18:11:31 worker-1 systemd[1]: Stopping kubelet: The Kubernetes
Node Agent...
Jan 20 18:11:31 worker-1 systemd[1]: Stopped kubelet: The Kubernetes Node Agent.
Jan 20 18:11:31 worker-1 systemd[1]: Started kubelet: The Kubernetes Node Agent.
....
```

You will want to restart the process once you have identified the issue in the logs and fixed it:

```
$ systemctl restart kubelet
```

Checking the certificate

Sometimes, the certificate used by the kubelet can expire. Make sure that the values for the attributes `Issuer` and `Not After` are correct:

```
$ openssl x509 -in /var/lib/kubelet/pki/kubelet.crt -text
Certificate:
    Data:
        Version: 3 (0x2)
        Serial Number: 2 (0x2)
        Signature Algorithm: sha256WithRSAEncryption
        Issuer: CN = worker-1-ca@1642702301
        Validity
            Not Before: Jan 20 17:11:41 2022 GMT
            Not After : Jan 20 17:11:41 2023 GMT
        Subject: CN = worker-1@1642702301
        ...
```

Checking the kube-proxy Pod

The kube-proxy components run in a set of dedicated Pods in the namespace `kube-system`. You can clearly identify the Pods by their naming prefix `kube-proxy` and the appended hash. Verify if any of the Pods states a different status than "Running." Each of the kube-proxy Pods runs on a dedicated worker node. You can add the `-o wide` option to render the node the Pod is running on in a new column:

```
$ kubectl get pods -n kube-system
NAME                    READY   STATUS    RESTARTS   AGE
...
kube-proxy-csrww        1/1     Running   0          4d22h
kube-proxy-fjd48        1/1     Running   0          4d22h
kube-proxy-tvf52        1/1     Running   0          4d22h
```

Take a look at the event log for kube-proxy Pods that seem to have an issue. The following command describes the Pod named kube-proxy-csrww. In addition, you might find more information in the event log of the corresponding DaemonSet:

```
$ kubectl describe pod kube-proxy-csrww -n kube-system
$ kubectl describe daemonset kube-proxy -n kube-system
```

The logs may come in handy as well. You will be able to check the logs only for the kube-proxy Pod that runs on the specific worker node:

```
$ kubectl describe pod kube-proxy-csrww -n kube-system | grep Node:
Node:                   worker-1/10.0.2.15
$ kubectl logs kube-proxy-csrww -n kube-system
```

Summary

As a Kubernetes administrator, you need to be capable of identifying and fixing application and cluster component issues.

Logging is essential for tracing application flows and capturing potential error messages. You can configure logging on a cluster level and a node level, each of which comes with its own benefits and potential drawbacks. Depending on the log capturing approach, aspects such as log rotation and logging backend service may be incorporated. On the Pod level, you can directly ask for the application logs using the kubectl logs command. Use the command-line option -c to target a specific container in a multi-container setup.

Kubernetes' native monitoring service, the metrics server, can be installed on the cluster to collect and aggregate Pod and node resource utilization data. Nodes send metrics via the kubelet to the centralized metrics server. End users can use the kubectl top command to render those metrics as a means to identify excessive resource usage.

Misconfiguration of workload and networking objects can lead to applications mishaps. You need to be familiar with the strategies relevant for diagnosing root causes and how fix them. A cluster may also develop error states leading to a variety of operational issues. You need to know which cluster components and processes run on control plane nodes and worker nodes. We discussed strategies for tackling different failure situations.

Exam Essentials

Understand logging configuration on a theoretical level

Kubernetes logging is not a built-in capability. You have to configure logging proactively on the cluster or the node level. Compare the different approaches and their potential trade-offs.

Make accessing container logs your daily bread and butter

Accessing container logs is straightforward. Simply use the `logs` command. Practice the use of all relevant command-line options. The option `-c` targets a specific container. The option does not have to be used explicitly for single-container Pods. The option `-f` tails the log entries if you want to see live processing in an application. The `-p` option can be used for accessing logs if the container needed to be restarted, but you still want to take a look at the previous container logs.

Install and use the metrics server

The metrics server isn't installed on a Kubernetes cluster by default. Go through the motions of installing the service. For the exam, you can assume that the metrics server is already available. Use the `top` command for Pods and nodes to identify resource consumption.

Know how to troubleshoot applications

Applications running in a Pod can easily break due to misconfiguration. Think of possible scenarios that can occur and try to model them proactively to represent a failure situation. Then using the commands `get`, `logs`, and `exec`, get to the bottom of the issue and fix it. Try to dream up obscure scenarios to become more comfortable with finding and fixing application issues for different resource types.

Know how to troubleshoot clusters

Control-plane and worker nodes can become unresponsive or dysfunctional for a variety of reasons. Administrators need to take care of their cluster's health in order to keep it operational and scalable. Try to emulate error scenarios that may occur and apply the discussed troubleshooting techniques to identify and fix the underlying root cause.

Sample Exercises

Solutions to these exercises are available in the Appendix.

1. You are supposed to implement cluster-level logging with a sidecar container. Create a multi-container Pod named `multi`. The main application container named `nginx` should use the image `nginx:1.21.6`. The sidecar container named

streaming uses the image busybox:1.35.0 and the arguments /bin/sh, -c, and 'tail -n+1 -f /var/log/nginx/access.log'.

2. Define a volume of type emptyDir for the Pod and mount it to the path /var/log/nginx for both containers.

3. Access the endpoint of the nginx service a couple of times using a wget or curl command. Inspect the logs of the sidecar container.

4. Create two Pods named stress-1 and stress-2. Define a container that uses the image polinux/stress:1.0.4 with the command stress and the arguments /bin/sh, -c, and 'stress --vm 1 --vm-bytes $(shuf -i 20-200 -n 1)M --vm-hang 1'. Set the container memory resource limits and requests to 250Mi.

5. Use the data available through the metrics server to identify which of the Pods, stress-1 or stress-2, consumes the most memory. Write the name of the Pod to the file max-memory.txt.

6. Navigate to the directory app-a/ch07/troubleshooting-pod of the checked-out GitHub repository *bmuschko/cka-study-guide* (*https://oreil.ly/jUIq8*). Follow the instructions in the file instructions.md (*https://oreil.ly/j9lTr*) for troubleshooting a faulty Pod setup.

7. Navigate to the directory app-a/ch07/troubleshooting-deployment of the checked-out GitHub repository *bmuschko/cka-study-guide* (*https://oreil.ly/jUIq8*). Follow the instructions in the file instructions.md for troubleshooting a faulty Deployment setup.

8. Navigate to the directory app-a/ch07/troubleshooting-service of the checked-out GitHub repository *bmuschko/cka-study-guide* (*https://oreil.ly/jUIq8*). Follow the instructions in the file instructions.md (*https://oreil.ly/Z9kou*) for troubleshooting a faulty Service setup.

9. Navigate to the directory app-a/ch07/troubleshooting-control-plane-node of the checked-out GitHub repository *bmuschko/cka-study-guide* (*https://oreil.ly/ jUIq8*). Follow the instructions in the file instructions.md (*https://oreil.ly/ lGygu*) for troubleshooting a faulty control plane node setup.

   Prerequisite: This exercise requires the installation of the tools Vagrant (*https:// oreil.ly/sasln*) and VirtualBox (*https://oreil.ly/9Cvg9*).

10. Navigate to the directory app-a/ch07/troubleshooting-worker-node of the checked-out GitHub repository *bmuschko/cka-study-guide* (*https://oreil.ly/jUIq8*). Follow the instructions in the file instructions.md (*https://oreil.ly/Kyh58*) for troubleshooting a faulty worker node setup.

    Prerequisite: This exercise requires the installation of the tools Vagrant (*https:// oreil.ly/sasln*) and VirtualBox (*https://oreil.ly/9Cvg9*).

## CHAPTER 8

Wrapping Up

Thanks for joining this whirlwind tour on anything that's relevant to the Certified Kubernetes Administrator certification. I condensed the most relevant information in this book for you to succeed. Your journey does not end here. In fact, it's only the beginning as there's so much more learn in the realm of Kubernetes. I would encourage you to dive deeper into the topics discussed in this book and branch out even further into the Kubernetes tooling ecosystem.

Before we conclude, let me summarize the most important points for acing the exam. The key for scoring as many points as possible is to practice, practice, practice. Run through the sample exercises in this book, tap into free and commercial practice exams, and even come up with your own practice scenarios to learn the ins and outs of Kubernetes and kubectl. To solidify your exposure to Kubernetes, read the Kubernetes documentation from start to end at least once. In the course of this book, we've seen that the exam is about more than just testing your knowledge of kubectl. You'll also need to be comfortable with other tools like vim, bash, and YAML.

I wish you all the best for acquiring the CKA certification. With this book, I hope I can give you the relevant information and learning strategies to succeed.

> For the things we have to learn before we can do them, we learn by doing them.
>
> —Aristotle

Answers to Review Questions

Chapter 2, "Cluster Architecture, Installation, and Configuration"

1. First, create the namespace named apps. Then, we'll create the ServiceAccount:

   ```
   $ kubectl create namespace apps
   $ kubectl create serviceaccount api-access -n apps
   ```

   Alternatively, you can use the declarative approach. Create the namespace from the definition in the file apps-namespace.yaml:

   ```
   apiVersion: v1
   kind: Namespace
   metadata:
     name: apps
   ```

   Create the namespace from the YAML file:

   ```
   $ kubectl create -f apps-namespace.yaml
   ```

   Create a new YAML file called api-serviceaccount.yaml with the following contents:

   ```
   apiVersion: v1
   kind: ServiceAccount
   metadata:
     name: api-access
     namespace: apps
   ```

   Run the create command to instantiate the ServiceAccount from the YAML file:

   ```
   $ kubectl create -f api-serviceaccount.yaml
   ```

2. Use the create clusterrole command to create the ClusterRole imperatively:

```
$ kubectl create clusterrole api-clusterrole --verb=watch,list,get \
  --resource=pods
```

If you'd rather start with the YAML file, use content shown in the file api-clusterrole.yaml:

```
apiVersion: rbac.authorization.k8s.io/v1
kind: ClusterRole
metadata:
  name: api-clusterrole
rules:
- apiGroups: [""]
  resources: ["pods"]
  verbs: ["watch","list","get"]
```

Create the ClusterRole from the YAML file:

```
$ kubectl create -f api-clusterrole.yaml
```

Use the create clusterrolebinding command to create the ClusterRoleBinding imperatively.

```
$ kubectl create clusterrolebinding api-clusterrolebinding \
  --serviceaccount=apps:api-access --clusterrole=api-clusterrole
```

The declarative approach of the ClusterRoleBinding could look like the one in the file api-clusterrolebinding.yaml:

```
apiVersion: rbac.authorization.k8s.io/v1
kind: ClusterRoleBinding
metadata:
  name: api-clusterrolebinding
roleRef:
  apiGroup: rbac.authorization.k8s.io
  kind: ClusterRole
  name: api-clusterrole
subjects:
- apiGroup: ""
  kind: ServiceAccount
  name: api-access
  namespace: apps
```

Create the ClusterRoleBinding from the YAML file:

```
$ kubectl create -f api-clusterrolebinding.yaml
```

3. Execute the run command to create the Pods in the different namespaces. You will need to create the namespace rm before you can instantiate the Pod disposable:

```
$ kubectl run operator --image=nginx:1.21.1 --restart=Never \
  --port=80 --serviceaccount=api-access -n apps
$ kubectl create namespace rm
```

```
$ kubectl run disposable --image=nginx:1.21.1 --restart=Never \
  -n rm
```

The following YAML manifest shows the `rm` namespace definition stored in the file `rm-namespace.yaml`:

```
apiVersion: v1
kind: Namespace
metadata:
  name: rm
```

The YAML representation of those Pods stored in the file `api-pods.yaml` could look as follows:

```
apiVersion: v1
kind: Pod
metadata:
  name: operator
  namespace: apps
spec:
  serviceAccountName: api-access
  containers:
  - name: operator
    image: nginx:1.21.1
    ports:
    - containerPort: 80
---
apiVersion: v1
kind: Pod
metadata:
  name: disposable
  namespace: rm
spec:
  containers:
  - name: disposable
    image: nginx:1.21.1
```

Create the namespace and Pods from the YAML files:

```
$ kubectl create -f rm-namespace.yaml
$ kubectl create -f api-pods.yaml
```

4. Determine the API server endpoint and the Secret access token of the ServiceAccount. You will need this information for making the API calls:

```
$ kubectl config view --minify -o \
  jsonpath='{.clusters[0].cluster.server}'
https://192.168.64.4:8443
$ kubectl get secret $(kubectl get serviceaccount api-access -n apps \
  -o jsonpath='{.secrets[0].name}') -o jsonpath='{.data.token}' -n apps \
  | base64 --decode
eyJhbGciOiJSUzI1NiIsImtpZCI6Ii1hOUhI...
```

Open an interactive shell to the Pod named operator:

```
$ kubectl exec operator -it -n apps -- /bin/sh
```

Emit API calls for listing all Pods and deleting the Pod disposable living in the rm namespace. You will find that while the list operation is permitted, the delete operation isn't:

```
# curl https://192.168.64.4:8443/api/v1/namespaces/rm/pods --header \
"Authorization: Bearer eyJhbGciOiJSUzI1NiIsImtpZCI6Ii1hOUhI..." \
--insecure
{
    "kind": "PodList",
    "apiVersion": "v1",
    ...
}
# curl -X DELETE https://192.168.64.4:8443/api/v1/namespaces \
/rm/pods/disposable --header \
"Authorization: Bearer eyJhbGciOiJSUzI1NiIsImtpZCI6Ii1hOUhI..." \
--insecure
{
  "kind": "Status",
  "apiVersion": "v1",
  "metadata": {

  },
  "status": "Failure",
  "message": "pods \"disposable\" is forbidden: User \
\"system:serviceaccount:apps:api-access\" cannot delete \
resource \"pods\" in
API group \"\" in the namespace \"rm\"",
  "reason": "Forbidden",
  "details": {
    "name": "disposable",
    "kind": "pods"
  },
  "code": 403
}
```

5. The solution to this sample exercise requires a lot of manual steps. The following commands do not render their output.

Open an interactive shell to the control plane node using Vagrant:

```
$ vagrant ssh k8s-control-plane
```

Upgrade kubeadm to version 1.21.2 and apply it:

```
$ sudo apt-mark unhold kubeadm && sudo apt-get update && sudo apt-get \
  install -y kubeadm=1.21.2-00 && sudo apt-mark hold kubeadm
$ sudo kubeadm upgrade apply v1.21.2
```

Drain the node, upgrade the kubelet and kubectl, restart the kubelet, and uncordon the node:

```
$ kubectl drain k8s-control-plane --ignore-daemonsets
$ sudo apt-get update && sudo apt-get install -y \
  --allow-change-held-packages kubelet=1.21.2-00 kubectl=1.21.2-00
$ sudo systemctl daemon-reload
$ sudo systemctl restart kubelet
$ kubectl uncordon k8s-control-plane
```

The version of the node should now say v1.21.2. Exit the node:

```
$ kubectl get nodes
$ exit
```

Open an interactive shell to the first worker node using Vagrant. Repeat all of the following steps for the other worker nodes:

```
$ vagrant ssh worker-1
```

Upgrade kubeadm to version 1.21.2 and apply it to the node:

```
$ sudo apt-get update && sudo apt-get install -y \
  --allow-change-held-packages kubeadm=1.21.2-00
$ sudo kubeadm upgrade node
```

Drain the node, upgrade the kubelet and kubectl, restart the kubelet, and uncordon the node:

```
$ kubectl drain worker-1 --ignore-daemonsets
$ sudo apt-get update && sudo apt-get install -y \
  --allow-change-held-packages kubelet=1.21.2-00 kubectl=1.21.2-00
$ sudo systemctl daemon-reload
$ sudo systemctl restart kubelet
$ kubectl uncordon worker-1
```

The version of the node should now say v1.21.2. Exit the node:

```
$ kubectl get nodes
$ exit
```

6. The solution to this sample exercise requires a lot of manual steps. The following commands do not render their output.

Open an interactive shell to the control plane node using Vagrant. That's not with the etcdctl command-line tool installed:

```
$ vagrant ssh k8s-control-plane
```

Determine the parameters of the Pod etcd-k8s-control-plane by describing it. Use the correct parameter values to create a snapshot file:

```
$ kubectl describe pod etcd-k8s-control-plane -n kube-system
$ sudo ETCDCTL_API=3 etcdctl --cacert=/etc/kubernetes/pki/etcd/ca.crt \
  --cert=/etc/kubernetes/pki/etcd/server.crt \
  --key=/etc/kubernetes/pki/etcd/server.key snapshot save /opt/etcd.bak
```

Restore the backup from the snapshot file. Edit the etcd YAML manifest and change the value of `spec.volumes.hostPath.path` for the volume named etcd-data:

```
$ sudo ETCDCTL_API=3 etcdctl --data-dir=/var/bak snapshot restore \
  /opt/etcd.bak
$ sudo vim /etc/kubernetes/manifests/etcd.yaml
```

After a short while, the Pod `etcd-k8s-control-plane` should transition back into the "Running" status. Exit the node:

```
$ kubectl get pod etcd-k8s-control-plane -n kube-system
$ exit
```

Chapter 3, "Workloads"

1. First, create the Deployment named `nginx`. Use the imperative approach for the fastest turnaround time:

   ```
   $ kubectl create deployment nginx --image=nginx:1.17.0 --replicas=2
   ```

2. The scale command increases the number of replicas to 7. The `get` command should render seven Pods with the Deployment's name as the prefix in their names:

   ```
   $ kubectl scale deployment nginx --replicas=7
   $ kubectl get deployments,pods
   NAME                       READY   UP-TO-DATE   AVAILABLE   AGE
   deployment.apps/nginx      7/7     7            7           93s

   NAME                            READY   STATUS    RESTARTS   AGE
   pod/nginx-844f997cc9-6tbzw      1/1     Running   0          93s
   pod/nginx-844f997cc9-8mzz2      1/1     Running   0          93s
   pod/nginx-844f997cc9-n7g8x      1/1     Running   0          10s
   pod/nginx-844f997cc9-sbrmf      1/1     Running   0          10s
   pod/nginx-844f997cc9-wtbk6      1/1     Running   0          10s
   pod/nginx-844f997cc9-xghl9      1/1     Running   0          10s
   pod/nginx-844f997cc9-zsggj      1/1     Running   0          10s
   ```

3. The API version of a Horizontal Pod Autoscaler that currently supports defining CPU and memory utilization thresholds is `autoscaling/v2beta2`. The following YAML manifest specifies the autoscaling parameters in the file `hpa.yaml`:

   ```
   apiVersion: autoscaling/v2beta2
   kind: HorizontalPodAutoscaler
   metadata:
     name: nginx-hpa
   spec:
     scaleTargetRef:
       apiVersion: apps/v1
       kind: Deployment
   ```

```
      name: nginx
    minReplicas: 3
    maxReplicas: 20
    metrics:
    - type: Resource
      resource:
        name: cpu
        target:
          type: Utilization
          averageUtilization: 65
    - type: Resource
      resource:
        name: memory
        target:
          type: AverageValue
          averageValue: 1Gi
```

Create the Horizontal Pod Autoscaler with the create command:

```
$ kubectl create -f hpa.yaml
```

4. You can either manually change the image name by editing the live object via the edit command or use the set image command as a shortcut. Use the --record option so that the command is recorded as the change cause:

```
$ kubectl set image deployment nginx nginx=nginx:1.21.1 --record
```

The rollout history will show two revisions, the starting revision 1 and the most recent change as 2. Notice that the change cause shows the recorded command:

```
$ kubectl rollout history deployment nginx
deployment.apps/nginx
REVISION   CHANGE-CAUSE
1          <none>
2          kubectl set image deployment nginx nginx=nginx:1.21.1 \
           --record=true
```

Use the rollout undo command to roll back to the previous revision. Revision 1 is turned into revision 3:

```
$ kubectl rollout undo deployment nginx --to-revision=1
$ kubectl rollout history deployment nginx
deployment.apps/nginx
REVISION   CHANGE-CAUSE
2          kubectl set image deployment nginx nginx=nginx:1.21.1 \
           --record=true
3          <none>
```

5. The following YAML manifest shows the Secret of type kubernetes.io/basic-auth in the file basic-auth-secret.yaml:

```
apiVersion: v1
kind: Secret
```

```
metadata:
  name: basic-auth
type: kubernetes.io/basic-auth
stringData:
  username: super
  password: my-s8cr3t
```

Create the Secret using the `create` command:

```
$ kubectl create -f basic-auth-secret.yaml
```

To mount the Secret as a volume to the Pod template, edit the live object of the Deployment using the `edit` command. The essential portions of the Deployment will look similar to the following YAML manifest:

```
apiVersion: apps/v1
kind: Deployment
metadata:
  name: nginx
  labels:
    app: nginx
spec:
  replicas: 7
  selector:
    matchLabels:
      app: nginx
  template:
    metadata:
      labels:
        app: nginx
    spec:
      containers:
      - name: nginx
        image: nginx:1.17.0
        volumeMounts:
        - mountPath: /etc/secret
          name: auth-vol
          readOnly: true
      volumes:
      - name: auth-vol
        secret:
          secretName: basic-auth
```

Chapter 4, "Scheduling and Tooling"

1. The manifest of a Pod that defines resource boundaries stored in a file `ingress-controller-pod.yaml` could look as follows:

```
apiVersion: v1
kind: Pod
```

```
metadata:
  name: ingress-controller
spec:
  containers:
  - name: ingress-controller
    image: bitnami/nginx-ingress-controller:1.0.0
    resources:
      requests:
        memory: "256Mi"
        cpu: "1"
      limits:
        memory: "1024Mi"
        cpu: "2.5"
```

2. Assume a cluster with three nodes: one control plane node and two worker nodes. The following multinode cluster has been set up with Minikube. For more information, see the setup instructions (*https://oreil.ly/nVhYn*):

```
$ kubectl get nodes
NAME          STATUS   ROLES                 AGE   VERSION
minikube      Ready    control-plane,master  41d   v1.21.2
minikube-m02  Ready    <none>                21h   v1.21.2
minikube-m03  Ready    <none>                21h   v1.21.2
```

You can identify which node runs the Pod after creating the object. Write the node name to the file node.txt:

```
$ kubectl create -f ingress-controller-pod.yaml
$ kubectl get pod ingress-controller -o yaml | grep nodeName:
  nodeName: minikube-m02
$ echo "minikube-m02" >> node.txt
```

3. Navigate to the folder containing the manifests directory. Create all objects contained in the manifests directory using the recursive apply command:

```
$ kubectl apply -f manifests/ -R
configmap/logs-config created
pod/nginx created
```

4. Modify the value of the key dir in the file configmap.yaml using an editor. Then update the live object of the ConfigMap using the following command:

```
$ vim manifests/configmap.yaml
$ kubectl apply -f manifests/configmap.yaml
configmap/logs-config configured
```

Delete all objects that have been created from the manifests directory using the recursive delete command:

```
$ kubectl delete -f manifests/ -R
configmap "logs-config" deleted
pod "nginx" deleted
```

5. Create the file kustomization.yaml. It should define the common attribute for the namespace and reference the resource with the file pod.yaml. The following YAML file shows its contents:

```
namespace: t012
resources:
- pod.yaml
```

Run the following kustomize command to render the transformed manifest as console output:

```
$ kubectl kustomize ./
apiVersion: v1
kind: Pod
metadata:
  name: nginx
  namespace: t012
spec:
  containers:
  - image: nginx:1.21.1
    name: nginx
```

Chapter 5, "Services and Networking"

1. Start by creating the namespace external. Within the namespace, create the Deployment and the Service using the imperative command:

```
$ kubectl create namespace external
$ kubectl create deployment nginx --image=nginx --port=80 --replicas=3 \
  -n external
$ kubectl create service loadbalancer nginx --tcp=80:80 -n external
```

If you'd rather use the declarative approach, see the following YAML manifests:

external-namespace.yaml:

```
apiVersion: v1
kind: Namespace
metadata:
  name: external
```

external-deployment.yaml:

```
apiVersion: apps/v1
kind: Deployment
metadata:
  name: nginx
  namespace: external
spec:
  selector:
    matchLabels:
      app: nginx
```

```
  template:
    metadata:
      labels:
        app: nginx
    spec:
      containers:
      - image: nginx
        name: nginx
        ports:
        - containerPort: 80
```

external-service.yaml:

```
apiVersion: v1
kind: Service
metadata:
  name: nginx
  namespace: external
spec:
  type: LoadBalancer
  selector:
    app: nginx
  ports:
  - port: 80
    targetPort: 80
```

To create all object, run the create or apply command:

```
$ kubectl create -f external-namespace.yaml
$ kubectl create -f external-deployment.yaml
$ kubectl create -f external-service.yaml
```

2. Determine the external IP address of the Service of type LoadBalancer. In the following output, the external IP address is 10.108.34.2. If you are using Minikube, remember to run minikube tunnel in another shell so that the value of EXTERNAL-IP gets populated:

```
$ kubectl get service -n external
NAME    TYPE          CLUSTER-IP    EXTERNAL-IP   PORT(S)       AGE
nginx   LoadBalancer  10.108.34.2   10.108.34.2   80:31898/TCP  36m
```

The following curl command makes a call to the Service using the external IP address and port:

```
$ wget 10.108.34.2:80
<!DOCTYPE html>
<html>
<head>
<title>Welcome to nginx!</title>
...
```

3. Edit the live object by changing the value of the attribute `spec.type` from LoadBalancer to ClusterIP:

```
$ kubectl edit service nginx -n external
...
spec:
  type: ClusterIP
...
```

The Service should indicate the type `ClusterIP` now. Notice that there's no more value for the external IP address. Furthermore, the statically assigned port is gone as well:

```
$ kubectl get service -n external
NAME     TYPE        CLUSTER-IP    EXTERNAL-IP   PORT(S)   AGE
nginx    ClusterIP   10.108.34.2   <none>        80/TCP    52m
```

A Service of type `ClusterIP` is accessible only from within the cluster. You can make a call to the Service from a temporary Pod in the same namespace. You can either use the cluster IP address (in this case 10.108.34.2) or use the DNS name for the Service nginx:

```
$ kubectl run tmp --image=busybox --restart=Never -n external -it --rm \
  -- wget 10.108.34.2:80
Connecting to 10.108.34.2:80 (10.108.34.2:80)
saving to 'index.html'
index.html           100% |*****************************|   615  \
0:00:00 ETA
'index.html' saved
pod "tmp" deleted
$ kubectl run tmp --image=busybox --restart=Never -n external -it --rm \
  -- wget nginx:80
Connecting to 10.108.34.2:80 (10.108.34.2:80)
saving to 'index.html'
index.html           100% |*****************************|   615  \
0:00:00 ETA
'index.html' saved
pod "tmp" deleted
```

4. To create the Ingress imperatively, run the following command:

```
$ kubectl create ingress incoming --rule="/*=nginx:80" -n external
```

If you'd rather use the declarative approach, see the YAML manifest in the file incoming-ingress.yaml shown here:

```
apiVersion: networking.k8s.io/v1
kind: Ingress
metadata:
  name: incoming
  namespace: external
spec:
```

```
    rules:
    - http:
        paths:
        - backend:
            service:
              name: nginx
              port:
                number: 80
          path: /
          pathType: Prefix
```

To create the object, run the create or apply command:

```
$ kubectl create -f incoming-ingress.yaml
```

5. To verify the correct behavior of the Ingress, retrieve the IP address of any node in the cluster. Here, we are dealing with only a single node that has the IP address 192.168.64.19:

```
$ kubectl get nodes -o wide
NAME       STATUS   ROLES                  AGE   VERSION   INTERNAL-IP   \
EXTERNAL-IP  OS-IMAGE               KERNEL-VERSION   CONTAINER-RUNTIME
minikube   Ready    control-plane,master   13d   v1.21.2   192.168.64.19 \
<none>       Buildroot 2020.02.12   4.19.182         docker://20.10.6
```

The Ingress is configured to access calls to any hostname. Make a call to the node's IP address from your local machine. The traffic will be routed to the Pods through the Service named nginx:

```
$ curl 192.168.64.19
<!DOCTYPE html>
<html>
<head>
<title>Welcome to nginx!</title>
...
```

6. For a fast turnaround, you can create the echoserver Pod and the Service together with the run command plus the --expose CLI option:

```
$ kubectl run echoserver --image=k8s.gcr.io/echoserver:1.10 \
  --restart=Never --port=8080 --expose -n external
```

The declarative approach requires the creation of the following YAML manifests:

external-echoserver-pod.yaml:

```
apiVersion: v1
kind: Pod
metadata:
  name: echoserver
  namespace: external
  labels:
    run: nginx
```

```
spec:
  containers:
  - name: echoserver
    image: k8s.gcr.io/echoserver:1.10
    ports:
    - containerPort: 8080
```

external-echoserver-service.yaml:

```
apiVersion: v1
kind: Service
metadata:
  name: echoserver
  namespace: external
spec:
  type: ClusterIP
  selector:
    run: nginx
  ports:
  - port: 8080
    targetPort: 8080
```

To create the object, run the create or apply command:

```
$ kubectl create -f external-echoserver-pod.yaml
$ kubectl create -f external-echoserver-service.yaml
```

Modify the existing Ingress and add a new rule that routes to the echoservice Service. The resulting YAML definition should look as follows:

```
apiVersion: networking.k8s.io/v1
kind: Ingress
metadata:
  name: incoming
  namespace: external
spec:
  rules:
  - http:
      paths:
      - backend:
          service:
            name: nginx
            port:
              number: 80
        path: /
        pathType: Prefix
      - backend:
          service:
            name: echoserver
            port:
              number: 8080
```

```
      path: /echo
      pathType: Exact
```

7. Make a call to the node's IP address from your local machine using the path /echo. The traffic will be routed to the Pods through the Service named echoservice:

```
$ curl 192.168.64.19/echo

Hostname: echoserver
...
```

8. You can customize CoreDNS settings by editing the ConfigMap coredns in the namespace kube-system using the command kubectl edit configmap coredns -n kube-system. The following YAML manifest shows the rewrite rule:

```
apiVersion: v1
kind: ConfigMap
metadata:
  name: coredns-custom
  namespace: kube-system
data:
  Corefile: |
    .:53 {
        ...
        rewrite name substring svc.cka.example.com svc.cluster.local
        kubernetes cluster.local in-addr.arpa ip6.arpa {
        ...
    }
```

Find the Pod running CoreDNS in the namespace kube-system and delete it to force a re-creation of the Pod. You should see that Kubernetes creates a new object for the CoreDNS Pod:

```
$ kubectl get pods -n kube-system
NAME                          READY   STATUS    RESTARTS   AGE
coredns-558bd4d5db-kjdtx      1/1     Running   0          9m35s
...
$ kubectl delete pod coredns-558bd4d5db-kjdtx -n kube-system
$ kubectl get pods -n kube-system
NAME                          READY   STATUS    RESTARTS   AGE
coredns-558bd4d5db-mc98t      1/1     Running   0          54s
...
```

9. Create the namespace hello if it doesn't exist yet. Run a wget command against echoserver.external.svc.cka.example.com from a temporary Pod in the hello namespace. The call should succeed:

```
$ kubectl create namespace hello
$ kubectl run tmp --image=busybox --restart=Never -n hello -it --rm \
    -- wget echoserver.external.svc.cka.example.com:8080
```

```
Connecting to echoserver.external.svc.cka.example.com:8080 \
(10.104.248.24:8080)
saving to 'index.html'
index.html          100% |*******************************|    \
460  0:00:00 ETA
'index.html' saved
pod "tmp" deleted
```

Chapter 6, "Storage"

1. Start by creating a new file named `logs-pv.yaml`. The contents could look as follows:

```
kind: PersistentVolume
apiVersion: v1
metadata:
  name: logs-pv
spec:
  capacity:
    storage: 2Gi
  accessModes:
    - ReadWriteOnce
    - ReadOnlyMany
  persistentVolumeReclaimPolicy: Delete
  storageClassName: ""
  hostPath:
    path: /tmp/logs
```

Create the PersistentVolume object and check on its status:

```
$ kubectl create -f logs-pv.yaml
persistentvolume/logs-pv created
$ kubectl get pv
NAME        CAPACITY    ACCESS MODES    RECLAIM POLICY    STATUS \
  CLAIM                 STORAGECLASS    REASON   AGE
logs-pv     2Gi         RWO,ROX         Delete            Bound  \
  default/logs-pvc                               16m
```

2. Create the file `logs-pvc.yaml` to define the PersistentVolumeClaim. The following YAML manifest shows its contents:

```
kind: PersistentVolumeClaim
apiVersion: v1
metadata:
  name: logs-pvc
spec:
  accessModes:
    - ReadWriteOnce
  storageClassName: ""
  resources:
```

```
      requests:
        storage: 1Gi
```

Create the PersistentVolumeClaim object and check on its status:

```
$ kubectl create -f logs-pvc.yaml
persistentvolumeclaim/logs-pvc created
$ kubectl get pvc
NAME         STATUS    VOLUME      CAPACITY    ACCESS MODES  \
  STORAGECLASS    AGE
logs-pvc     Bound     logs-pv     2Gi         RWO,ROX       \
                       17m
```

3. Create the basic YAML manifest using the --dry-run command-line option:

```
$ kubectl run nginx --image=nginx --dry-run=client --restart=Never \
-o yaml > nginx-pod.yaml
```

Now, edit the file nginx-pod.yaml and bind the PersistentVolumeClaim to it:

```
apiVersion: v1
kind: Pod
metadata:
  creationTimestamp: null
  labels:
    run: nginx
  name: nginx
spec:
  volumes:
    - name: logs-volume
      persistentVolumeClaim:
        claimName: logs-pvc
  containers:
  - image: nginx
    name: nginx
    volumeMounts:
      - mountPath: "/var/log/nginx"
        name: logs-volume
    resources: {}
  dnsPolicy: ClusterFirst
  restartPolicy: Never
status: {}
```

Create the Pod using the following command and check its status:

```
$ kubectl create -f nginx-pod.yaml
pod/nginx created
$ kubectl get pods
NAME    READY    STATUS     RESTARTS    AGE
nginx   1/1      Running    0           8s
```

4. Use the exec command to open an interactive shell to the Pod and create a file in the mounted directory:

```
$ kubectl exec nginx -it -- /bin/sh
# cd /var/log/nginx
# touch my-nginx.log
# ls
access.log  error.log  my-nginx.log
# exit
```

5. Delete the Pod and the PersistentVolumeClaim. The PersistentVolume will be deleted automatically due to its reclaim policy:

```
$ kubectl delete pod nginx
$ kubectl delete pvc logs-pvc
$ kubectl get pv,pvc
No resources found
```

6. You can list the storage classes with the following command. If you are using Minikube, you will likely find only a single storage class, the default one. The existing storage class is named standard and uses the provisioner k8s.io/minikube-hostpath:

```
$ kubectl get sc
NAME                 PROVISIONER               RECLAIMPOLICY \
   VOLUMEBINDINGMODE  ALLOWVOLUMEEXPANSION   AGE
standard (default)   k8s.io/minikube-hostpath  Delete        \
   Immediate          false                  22d
```

7. Create the file custom-sc.yaml for the storage class. The YAML manifest could look as follows:

```
apiVersion: storage.k8s.io/v1
kind: StorageClass
metadata:
  name: custom
provisioner: k8s.io/minikube-hostpath
```

Create the storage class using the following command. Listing all storage classes renders the default storage class and the new one:

```
$ kubectl create -f custom-sc.yaml
storageclass.storage.k8s.io/custom created
$ kubectl get sc
NAME                 PROVISIONER               RECLAIMPOLICY \
   VOLUMEBINDINGMODE  ALLOWVOLUMEEXPANSION   AGE
custom               k8s.io/minikube-hostpath  Delete        \
   Immediate          false                  11s
standard (default)   k8s.io/minikube-hostpath  Delete        \
   Immediate          false                  22d
```

8. Create the file custom-pvc.yaml to define the PersistentVolumeClaim. The following YAML manifest shows its contents:

```
kind: PersistentVolumeClaim
apiVersion: v1
```

```
metadata:
  name: custom-pvc
spec:
  accessModes:
    - ReadWriteOnce
  storageClassName: custom
  resources:
    requests:
      storage: 500Mi
```

Create the PersistentVolumeClaim object and check on its status:

```
$ kubectl create -f custom-pvc.yaml
persistentvolumeclaim/custom-pvc created
$ kubectl get pv,pvc
NAME                                                           CAPACITY \
  ACCESS MODES   RECLAIM POLICY   STATUS   CLAIM       STORAGECLASS \
    REASON     AGE
persistentvolume/pvc-6fe081b5-e425-45cd-a94a-3488ce24cb87   500Mi    \
  RWO            Delete           Bound    default/custom-pvc   custom \
                 13s

NAME                                  STATUS \
  VOLUME                                         CAPACITY   ACCESS MODES \
    STORAGECLASS   AGE
persistentvolumeclaim/custom-pvc    Bound  \
  pvc-6fe081b5-e425-45cd-a94a-3488ce24cb87     500Mi      RWO \
            custom           13s
```

9. Write the name of the PersistentVolume to the file pv-name.txt:

```
$ echo "pvc-6fe081b5-e425-45cd-a94a-3488ce24cb87" > pv-name.txt
```

10. Deleting the PersistentVolumeClaim will delete the bound PersistentVolume as well:

```
$ kubectl delete pvc custom-pvc
$ kubectl get pv,pvc
No resources found
```

Chapter 7, "Troubleshooting"

1. Start by creating a YAML starting point for the Pod in the file named multi-container.yaml. The following command creates the file:

```
$ kubectl run multi --image=nginx:1.21.6 -o yaml --dry-run=client \
  --restart=Never > multi-container.yaml
```

Edit the YAML manifest. Add the sidecar container. The contents of the YAML file could look as follows:

```
apiVersion: v1
kind: Pod
metadata:
  name: multi
spec:
  containers:
  - image: nginx:1.21.6
    name: nginx
  - image: busybox:1.35.0
    name: streaming
    args: [/bin/sh, -c, 'tail -n+1 -f /var/log/nginx/access.log']
```

2. Add the volume definition and mount it to both containers. The final YAML manifest is shown here:

```
apiVersion: v1
kind: Pod
metadata:
  name: multi
spec:
  containers:
  - image: nginx:1.21.6
    name: nginx
    volumeMounts:
    - name: accesslog
      mountPath: /var/log/nginx
  - image: busybox:1.35.0
    name: streaming
    args: [/bin/sh, -c, 'tail -n+1 -f /var/log/nginx/access.log']
    volumeMounts:
    - name: accesslog
      mountPath: /var/log/nginx
  volumes:
  - name: accesslog
    emptyDir: {}
```

Create the Pod by pointing the `create` command to the YAML file:

```
$ kubectl create -f multi-container.yaml
```

3. Determine the IP address of the Pod. In the following example, the IP address is 10.244.2.3. Make three calls to nginx using a temporary Pod. The logs of the streaming container has three entries:

```
$ kubectl get pod multi -o wide
NAME     READY   STATUS    RESTARTS   AGE     IP           NODE          \
  NOMINATED NODE   READINESS GATES
multi    2/2     Running   0          3m23s   10.244.2.3   minikube-m03 \
  <none>          <none>
$ kubectl run tmp --image=busybox --restart=Never -it --rm \
  -- wget 10.244.2.3
$ kubectl run tmp --image=busybox --restart=Never -it --rm \
```

```
   -- wget 10.244.2.3
$ kubectl run tmp --image=busybox --restart=Never -it --rm \
   -- wget 10.244.2.3
$ kubectl logs multi -c streaming
10.244.1.2 - - [27/Jan/2022:16:44:25 +0000] "GET / HTTP/1.1" 200 \
615 "-" "Wget" "-"
10.244.1.3 - - [27/Jan/2022:16:44:29 +0000] "GET / HTTP/1.1" 200 \
615 "-" "Wget" "-"
10.244.1.4 - - [27/Jan/2022:16:44:32 +0000] "GET / HTTP/1.1" 200 \
615 "-" "Wget" "-"
```

4. Create the Pods `stress-1` and `stress-2`. The following YAML manifest shows the definition for the Pod named `stress-1` in the file `stress-1-pod.yaml`. Create a second YAML file and change the Pod name accordingly:

```
apiVersion: v1
kind: Pod
metadata:
  name: stress-1
spec:
  containers:
  - image: polinux/stress:1.0.4
    name: consumer
    resources:
      limits:
        memory: "250Mi"
      requests:
        memory: "250Mi"
    args: [/bin/sh, -c, 'stress --vm 1 --vm-bytes \
           $(shuf -i 20-200 -n 1)M --vm-hang 1']
```

Create the Pods and check their status:

```
$ kubectl create -f stress-1-pod.yaml
$ kubectl create -f stress-2-pod.yaml
$ kubectl get pods
NAME       READY   STATUS    RESTARTS   AGE
stress-1   1/1     Running   0          15m
stress-2   1/1     Running   0          6m28s
```

5. Install the metrics server (*https://oreil.ly/e1NSC*) if it isn't already available on your cluster. Retrieve the metrics for the Pods from the metrics server. In the example below, the Pod named `stress-2` consumes more memory. Write the name of the Pod the file *max-memory.txt*:

```
$ kubectl top pods
NAME       CPU(cores)   MEMORY(bytes)
stress-1   32m          93Mi
stress-2   47m          117Mi
$ echo "stress-2" > max-memory.txt
```

6. You can find the solution in the file *app-a/ch07/troubleshooting-pod/solution/solution.md* of the checked-out GitHub repository *bmuschko/cka-study-guide* (*https://oreil.ly/jUIq8*).

7. You can find the solution in the file *app-a/ch07/troubleshooting-deployment/solution/solution.md* of the checked-out GitHub repository *bmuschko/cka-study-guide* (*https://oreil.ly/jUIq8*).

8. You can find the solution in the file *app-a/ch07/troubleshooting-service/solution/solution.md* of the checked-out GitHub repository *bmuschko/cka-study-guide* (*https://oreil.ly/jUIq8*).

9. You can find the solution in the file *app-a/ch07/troubleshooting-control-plane-node/solution/solution.md* of the checked-out GitHub repository *bmuschko/cka-study-guide* (*https://oreil.ly/jUIq8*).

10. You can find the solution in the file *app-a/ch07/troubleshooting-worker-node/solution/solution.md* of the checked-out GitHub repository *bmuschko/cka-study-guide* (*https://oreil.ly/jUIq8*).

Index

S

X

X.509 client certificate, 15

Y

YAML

about, 6
merging files, 89
yq tool, 88
yq tool, 88

About the Author

Benjamin Muschko is a software engineer, consultant, and trainer with more than 20 years of experience in the industry. He's passionate about project automation, testing, and continuous delivery. Ben is an author, a frequent speaker at conferences, and an avid open source advocate. He holds the CKA and CKAD certifications.

Software projects sometimes feel like climbing a mountain. In his free time, Ben loves hiking Colorado's 14ers (*https://www.14ers.com*) and enjoys conquering long-distance trails.

Colophon

The animal on the cover of *Certified Kubernetes Administrator (CKA) Study Guide* is a Bengal eagle owl *(Bubo bengalensis)*, also known as the Indian eagle owl. They are a large horned-owl species native to the Indian subcontinent.

Bengal eagle owls are very similar to Eurasian eagle owls and may actually be a subspecies. They are a mixture of brown, grey, black, and white. They favor forests and rocky areas with scrub and brush. Their diet is primarily rodents and birds.

The owls breed from November to April, with females laying 2 to 4 eggs that incubate for about 35 days. The nest site is on the ground and is reused from year to year. As with other owls, Bengal eagle owls are nocturnal and known for their night calls. They are considered birds of ill omen and it is said that when their calls are delivered from high above, the call foretells death.

The Bengal eagle owl's conservation status is Least Concern. Many of the animals on O'Reilly covers are endangered; all of them are important to the world.

The cover illustration is by Karen Montgomery, based on an antique line engraving from *British Birds*. The cover fonts are Gilroy Semibold and Guardian Sans. The text font is Adobe Minion Pro; the heading font is Adobe Myriad Condensed; and the code font is Dalton Maag's Ubuntu Mono.

Milton Keynes UK
Ingram Content Group UK Ltd.
UKHW052003240924
448803UK00002B/2